Technology
and the Civil War

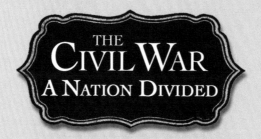

THE
CIVIL WAR
A NATION DIVIDED

A NATION DIVIDED

Technology
and the Civil War

Shane Mountjoy, Ph.D.

CHELSEA HOUSE
PUBLISHERS
An imprint of Infobase Publishing

TECHNOLOGY AND THE CIVIL WAR

Chelsea House
An imprint of Infobase Publishing
132 West 31st Street
New York, NY 10001

Library of Congress Cataloging-in-Publication Data
Mountjoy, Shane, 1967–
  Technology and the Civil War / by Shane Mountjoy.
      p. cm. — (The Civil War : a nation divided)
  Includes bibliographical references and index.
  ISBN 978-1-60413-037-9 (hardcover)
  1. United States—History—Civil War, 1861–1865—Technology. 2. Technology
—United States—History—19th century. I. Title.

  E468.9.M93 2009
  973.7'301—dc22   2008026563

Chelsea House books are available at special discounts when purchased in bulk quantities for businesses, associations, institutions, or sales promotions. Please call our Special Sales Department in New York at (212) 967-8800 or (800) 322-8755.

You can find Chelsea House on the World Wide Web at
http://www.chelseahouse.com

Series design by Lina Farinella
Cover design by Takeshi Takahashi

Printed in the United States of America

NMSG Bang 10 9 8 7 6 5 4 3 2 1

This book is printed on acid-free paper.

All links and Web addresses were checked and verified to be correct at the time of publication. Because of the dynamic nature of the Web, some addresses and links may have changed since publication and may no longer be valid.

Contents

Chronology

1820   The Missouri Compromise allows Maine to be admitted to the Union as a free state and Missouri as a slave state in 1821.

1831   William Lloyd Garrison publishes the first issue of his abolitionist newspaper, *The Liberator*.

1836   The House of Representatives passes a gag rule that automatically tables or postpones action on all petitions relating to slavery without hearing them.

1838   The Underground Railroad is formally organized.

1845   Former slave Frederick Douglass publishes his autobiography, *Narrative of the Life of Frederick Douglass, An American Slave*.

1850   Congress enacts several measures that together make up the Compromise of 1850.

1852   Harriet Beecher Stowe publishes *Uncle Tom's Cabin*.

1854   Congress passes the Kansas-Nebraska Act, which overturns the Missouri Compromise and thus opens northern territories to slavery.

1855   As Kansas prepares to vote, thousands of Border Ruffians from Missouri enter the territory in an attempt to influence the elections. This begins the period known as Bleeding Kansas.

1856   South Carolina representative Preston Brooks attacks Massachusetts senator Charles Sumner on the Senate floor and beats him with a cane.

1857   The Supreme Court rules, in *Dred Scott v. Sandford*, that blacks are not U.S. citizens and slaveholders have the right to take slaves into free areas of the country.

1859   John Brown seizes the arsenal at Harpers Ferry, Virginia. Robert E. Lee, then a Federal Army regular, leads the troops that capture Brown.

1860   **NOVEMBER**   Abraham Lincoln is elected president.

DECEMBER   A South Carolina convention passes an ordinance of secession, and the state secedes from the Union.

1861   **JANUARY**   Florida, Alabama, Georgia, and Louisiana secede from the Union.

FEBRUARY   Texas votes to secede from the Union. The Confederate States of America is formed and elects Jefferson Davis as its president.

MARCH   Abraham Lincoln is sworn in as the sixteenth president of the United States and delivers his first inaugural address.

APRIL 12   At 4:30 A.M., Confederate forces fire on South Carolina's Fort Sumter. The Civil War begins. Virginia secedes from the Union five days later.

MAY   Arkansas and North Carolina secede from the Union.

JUNE   Tennessee secedes from the Union.

JULY 21   The Union suffers a defeat in northern Virginia, at the First Battle of Bull Run (Manassas).

AUGUST   The Confederates win the Battle of Wilson's Creek, in Missouri.

1862   **FEBRUARY 6**   In Tennessee, Union general Ulysses S. Grant captures Fort Henry. Ten days later, he captures Fort Donelson.

MARCH The Confederate ironclad ship CSS *Virginia* (formerly the USS *Merrimack*) battles the Union ironclad *Monitor* to a draw. The Union's Peninsular Campaign begins in Virginia.

APRIL 6–7 Ulysses S. Grant defeats Confederate forces in the Battle of Shiloh (Pittsburg Landing), in Tennessee.

APRIL 24 David Farragut moves his fleet of Union Navy vessels up the Mississippi River to take New Orleans.

MAY 31 The Battle of Seven Pines (Fair Oaks) takes place in Virginia.

JUNE 1 Robert E. Lee assumes command of the Army of Northern Virginia.

JUNE 25–JULY 1 The Seven Days Battles are fought in Virginia.

AUGUST 29–30 The Union is defeated at the Second Battle of Bull Run.

SEPTEMBER 17 The bloodiest day in U.S. military history: Confederate forces under Robert E. Lee are stopped at Antietam, Maryland, by Union forces under George B. McClellan.

SEPTEMBER 22 The first Emancipation Proclamation to free slaves in the rebellious states is issued by President Lincoln.

DECEMBER 13 The Union's Army of the Potomac, under Ambrose Burnside, suffers a costly defeat at Fredericksburg, Virginia.

1863 **JANUARY 1** President Lincoln issues the final Emancipation Proclamation.

JANUARY 29 Ulysses S. Grant is placed in command of the Army of the West, with orders to capture Vicksburg, Mississippi.

MAY 1–4 Union forces under Joseph Hooker are defeated decisively by Robert E. Lee's much smaller forces at the Battle of Chancellorsville, in Virginia.

MAY 10 The South suffers a huge blow as General Thomas "Stonewall" Jackson dies from wounds he received during the battle of Chancellorsville.

JUNE 3 Robert E. Lee launches his second invasion of the North; he heads into Pennsylvania with 75,000 Confederate troops.

JULY 1–3 The tide of war turns against the South as the Confederates are defeated at the Battle of Gettysburg in Pennsylvania.

JULY 4 Vicksburg, the last Confederate stronghold on the Mississippi River, surrenders to Ulysses S. Grant after a six-week siege.

JULY 13–16 Antidraft riots rip through New York City.

JULY 18 The black 54th Massachusetts Infantry Regiment under Colonel Robert Gould Shaw assaults a fortified Confederate position at Fort Wagner, South Carolina.

SEPTEMBER 19–20 A decisive Confederate victory takes place at Chickamauga, Tennessee.

NOVEMBER 19 President Lincoln delivers the Gettysburg Address.

NOVEMBER 23–25 Ulysses S. Grant's Union forces win an important victory at the Battle of Chattanooga, in Tennessee.

1864

MARCH 9 President Lincoln names Ulysses S. Grant general-in-chief of all the armies of the United States.

MAY 4 Ulysses S. Grant opens a massive, coordinated campaign against Robert E. Lee's Confederate armies in Virginia.

MAY 5–6 The Battle of the Wilderness is fought in Virginia.

MAY 8–12   The Battle of Spotsylvania is fought in Virginia.

JUNE 1–3   The Battle of Cold Harbor is fought in Virginia.

JUNE 15   Union forces miss an opportunity to capture Petersburg, Virginia; this results in a nine-month Union siege of the city.

SEPTEMBER 2   Atlanta, Georgia, is captured by Union forces led by William Tecumseh Sherman.

OCTOBER 19   Union general Philip H. Sheridan wins a decisive victory over Confederate general Jubal Early in the Shenandoah Valley of Virginia.

NOVEMBER 8   Abraham Lincoln is reelected president, defeating Democratic challenger George B. McClellan.

NOVEMBER 15   General William T. Sherman begins his March to the Sea from Atlanta.

DECEMBER 15–16   Confederate general John Bell Hood is defeated at Nashville, Tennessee, by Union forces under George H. Thomas.

DECEMBER 21   General Sherman reaches Savannah, Georgia; he leaves behind a path of destruction 300 miles long and 60 miles wide from Atlanta to the sea.

1865   Southern states begin to pass Black Codes.

JANUARY 31   The U.S. Congress approves the Thirteenth Amendment to the United States Constitution.

FEBRUARY 3   A peace conference takes place as President Lincoln meets with Confederate Vice President Alexander Stephens at Hampton Roads, Virginia; the meeting ends in failure, and the war continues.

MARCH 4   Lincoln delivers his second inaugural address ("With Malice Toward None"). Congress establishes the Freedmen's Bureau.

MARCH 25   Robert E. Lee's Army of Northern Virginia begins its last offensive with an attack on the center of

Ulysses S. Grant's forces at Petersburg, Virginia. Four hours later, Lee's attack is broken.

APRIL 2 Grant's forces begin a general advance and break through Lee's lines at Petersburg. Lee evacuates Petersburg. Richmond, Virginia, the Confederate capital, is evacuated.

APRIL 9 Robert E. Lee surrenders his Confederate Army to Ulysses S. Grant at the village of Appomattox Court House, Virginia.

APRIL 14 John Wilkes Booth shoots President Lincoln at Ford's Theatre in Washington, D.C.

APRIL 15 President Abraham Lincoln dies. Vice President Andrew Johnson assumes the presidency.

APRIL 18 Confederate general Joseph E. Johnston surrenders to Union general William T. Sherman in North Carolina.

APRIL 26 John Wilkes Booth is shot and killed in a tobacco barn in Virginia.

DECEMBER The Thirteenth Amendment is ratified.

1866 Congress approves the Fourteenth Amendment to the Constitution.

Congress passes the Civil Rights Act.

The responsibilities and powers of the Freedmen's Bureau are expanded by Congress. The legislation is vetoed by President Johnson, but Congress overrides his veto.

The Ku Klux Klan is established in Tennessee.

1867 Congress passes the Military Reconstruction Act.

Congress passes the Tenure of Office Act.

1868 The impeachment trial of President Andrew Johnson ends in acquittal.

Ulysses S. Grant is elected president.

1869   Congress approves the Fifteenth Amendment to the Constitution.

1871   The Ku Klux Klan Act is passed by Congress.

1872   President Grant is reelected.

1875   A new Civil Rights Act is passed.

1877   Rutherford B. Hayes assumes the presidency.
        The Reconstruction Era ends.

Waging a War
with Technology

T he Greek philosopher Plato once wrote, "Necessity is the mother of invention." In war, conditions often create unforeseen necessities that require inventions, and the U.S. Civil War is no exception. It produced unique circumstances that required unique solutions, but it is perhaps the way in which the old and the new blended together that gives the Civil War its distinctive essence.

During the four years of war, Americans on both sides simultaneously reached backward to draw on past ways of doing things and forward to the future to gain an edge in the conflict. Unionists and Confederates alike drew from the ancient and the modern in their pursuit of victory. In many ways, the war was as much a clash of the traditional versus the newfangled as it was a collision of two ideologies. Nowhere is this clash more evident than in technology.

Both armies still relied upon mounted cavalry, an essential component of fighting forces since ancient times. Both sides, however, also made use of railroads and telegraphs—advances that had not existed just a generation earlier. The Union and Confederate navies used wooden sailing ships, but also constructed ironclads and even experimented with submarines. Some soldiers carried smoothbore muskets; others carried repeating rifles. Artillery ammunition varied from solid-shot cannonballs to exploding canisters. Cavalrymen used repeating revolvers with modified percussion caps (the devices that set off the guns' explosive charge) for easier reloading and firing but also carried steel sabers. Thus, despite the great technological advances made in the first half of the nineteenth century, combatants in the Civil War made use of both older and newer weapons and equipment.

In some respects, the Civil War was the result of advances made in technology. The American system of slavery was a costly one. To observers in the late eighteenth century, slavery appeared destined to die out after 1800. In 1793, however, the invention of the cotton gin—a machine that separated the seeds and hulls from the soft fibers of cotton—by Eli Whitney allowed slavery to become profitable again. In the past, many workers had been needed to pluck out the seeds by hand. With a cotton gin, fewer workers were needed for this kind of work—but now plantation owners saw the opportunity to raise and sell a cash crop, and northern businessmen saw the opportunity to make money by processing the cotton into fabric and clothing.

In the nearly seven decades between the introduction of the cotton gin and the start of the Civil War, the two regions of the country became increasingly defined by their economies. The South relied more and more on slavery to raise cash crops such as cotton and tobacco. Meanwhile, the North became industrialized. Factories sprang up to process cotton. Other factories turned out items that were mass-produced by machines that were powered first by water and later by steam. In the South, such things as rank, honor, and social status grew in importance. The foundation of economic, social, and political power in Southern society was slavery. During the same period,

The explosion of slavery in the South can be attributed to the development of the cotton gin, a machine that transformed regional cotton production into a profitable national industry. By eliminating the laborious process of manually removing cottonseeds from the precious fibers, cotton farmers in the South were able to double the amount of production every decade after the invention of the cotton gin. Above, an illustration of slaves using the first cotton gin.

Northern society increasingly centered on equality, as large numbers of Europeans came to the United States to build new lives. Many of these immigrants settled in Northern cities and found work in Northern factories. It was hardly possible for the two societies to be less alike.

The U.S. Civil War is unique for several reasons. Although in many respects the war was fought in much the same way that wars always had been fought, a new concept called "total war" altered the nature of the fighting. Northern military commanders such as William T. Sherman and Philip Sheridan considered the civilian population to be legitimate military targets. Sherman believed that war was anything but desirable and he intended to convince the South of the accuracy of his view. Civilians living in Georgia and South Carolina faced the wrath of the advancing Union Army during the summer and fall of 1864. The total war waged by Sherman's army left thousands of civilians homeless and ruined the Southern economy.

The nature of war was changed in more than just the minds and plans of political and military leaders, however. Technological advances helped alter civilian attitudes about the nature of war. Historian Charles D. Ross explains that as war changed during the course of the Civil War, everyday life did also:

> As the nature of war changed from 1861–1865, another transition from old to new was occurring in a broader sense. If one looks sixty years on either side of 1860, the differences in the typical human's way of life are astounding. In 1800, people traveled on foot, on horseback, or across the water by sail. Information traveled from place to place by the same slow methods.

From the dawn of the nineteenth century to 1860, humankind expanded its understanding of science. Inventors learned how to harness the power of steam. Other people developed ways to mass-produce manufactured items. Americans living in 1860 were not part of a mass-consumption society, but they did live in an economy that was capable of mass production. In 1800, individual skilled workers had produced firearms, clothing, and shoes and milled grain into flour. In 1860, factories churned out many of these same products, and they did so in ever-greater numbers.

The Springfield Arsenal in Massachusetts produced firearms for the federal government before and during the war. The Tredegar Ironworks in Richmond, Virginia, provided the Confederate Army with cannons, iron plating for ships, and other weapons. Changes in the U.S. economy in the 60 years between

1800 and the war produced the weapons, equipment, food, and transportation devices that enabled the North and South to wage war as they did from 1861 to1865. Many of the new technologies used in the war were available because of the rise in factories that mass-produced the products of those technological innovations. Ross goes on to describe the life of Americans six decades after 1860:

> By 1920 the development of the steam engine's successor, the internal combustible engine, had revolutionized transportation. The automobile was becoming available at affordable prices, airplanes were no longer a curiosity, and the Germans had already terrorized enemy forces with swarms of submarines. Household electricity was

Eli Whitney

Eli Whitney was an American inventor from New England. In 1792, Whitney traveled to Georgia and South Carolina. When he returned to Connecticut, he set out to create a machine to sell to plantation owners. Raw cotton contains seeds within the fluffy white fiber. Growers had to remove the seeds before they sold the crop. Removing the seeds required large amounts of labor. Whitney developed a series of mechanical wheels with brushes and wire screens to remove the seeds from the cotton. Growers who used this hand-powered engine could accomplish more work in less time with fewer workers. *Gin* is short for engine, and Whitney's invention is referred to as the cotton gin.

Whitney's invention led to the increased value of cotton in the Southern economy. Cotton became more profitable at the very time that tobacco profits were falling. Many plantation owners avoided purchasing Whitney's gin. Instead, they built their own being taken for granted and information now traveled at the speed of light: the telegram was already giving way to the "wireless," or radio. The first television was less than a decade away, the first atomic bomb only two decades into the future.

The Civil War was fought in the midst of an amazing shift in the way humans lived their lives. This shift included fundamental changes in routines of daily life that had existed since the earliest human civilizations. With the changes, Americans began to experience life in ways much like the ways of our modern world. In view of the fact that the Civil War took place at the same time as these larger changes, it is no surprise that the conflict served as a proving ground for various new

versions of the machine. Either way, the use of the cotton gin led to widespread changes in the Southern economy in the 60 years before the Civil War. In each decade leading up to the war, cotton production in the South doubled. This allowed the United States to account for three-fourths of the world's production of raw cotton each year. By 1850, the South supplied 60 percent of America's exports, most of it in cotton.

Whitney never made much profit from the cotton gin. In 1798, he analyzed how firearms were made. Making a gun was a long and difficult process. Skilled artisans made each part of a firearm by hand, and no two guns were exactly alike. Whitney figured out how to use machines to make standardized gun parts that could be interchanged with one another. Although it took several years for gun manufacturers to put his idea into practice, other industries began to use the concept almost immediately. Soon, manufacturers employed machines to produce tools, equipment, and other machines that featured standardized sizes and interchangeable parts. Whitney's technological contributions helped the North and the South develop their own unique economies.

The Civil War occurred in the middle of an incredible technological shift that pushed the North and South to combine old and new forms of combat. Cavalry were required to carry an old-fashioned saber and a newly-developed pistol in combat. Above, the camp of the Pennsylvania Cavalry in 1864.

technologies. People on each side tried to find and make use of any advantage to advance their cause. The use of technology and the method of fighting explain why the Civil War is sometimes called the first modern war.

Historian James M. McPherson argues, however, that analysis of the war places the conflict with earlier wars rather than modern wars. McPherson writes,

> But in many respects the Civil War was more traditional than modern—that is, it more closely resembled the Napoleonic Wars of fifty years earlier than World War I a half-century later. Despite railroads and steamboats, the armies still depended on animal-powered transport for

field supply. Campaigning slowed or halted during the winter and during heavy rains because of what Napoleon had once called the "fifth element" in war—mud. Despite advances in repeating arms and in rifling, most infantry-men carried muzzleloaders, and during the war's first year most of these were smoothbores. The cavalry was still an important military arm. The modern concept of substitut-ing firepower for men was yet in its infancy. Weapons and machines counted for much in this war—but men and horses still counted for more.

The Union and the Confederacy fought an epic struggle to de-termine which side's vision of America was going to guide the future of the nation. Each army fought this contest with one foot placed squarely in traditions of the past and the other planted firmly in the hope and expectation that new technologies held the key to victory. Despite the advances in technology, nations still needed men to wage war. In the midst of the large tech-nological and industrial transformation that affected America, the human sacrifice required in war remained. The changes in technology merely served to increase the levels of sacrifice demanded.

The industrial capabilities necessary to equip and transport soldiers relied on technology. The North held a decided advan-tage over the South in industrial capabilities. This advantage was evident when the war began, but it became more pronounced as the war dragged on. Technological advances in industry altered not only the nature of war, but also the size of the war. The be-ginning of hostilities created an overnight need for the United States to have a large military. In 1861, there were only 16,000 soldiers in the U.S. Army. By 1865, that number had reached one million soldiers. Historian John E. Clark Jr. notes that, "the Union achieved the most rapid mobilization in American his-tory." As the numbers of enlisted men increased, the volume of needed goods and supplies also increased. Soldiers needed uni-forms, belts, shoes, hats, firearms, ammunition, rucksacks, and dozens of other items. Armies needed food, blankets, tents, and other basics to fight in the field. The simple act of waging a war of such size is evidence of America's technological capabilities. The North filled these needs. They sometimes filled them slowly, but they filled them nonetheless.

Because the North held industrial and technological advantages, the Union was better equipped to deal with the changing face of war. Northern factories had the capability to meet the demands of an industrialized army. Before the war, the South relied on Northern manufacturing for many common products. During the war, without Northern goods, the South could hardly feed and clothe its own people, at home or on the front. In some respects, the outcome of the war was only a matter of time. That is not to say that the South could not have won. Rather, the North held enough of an advantage that the South faced an uphill battle. Although both sides benefited from the use of technology, the North and the South also struggled to find effective ways to use new knowledge, new machines, and new weapons. The story of the Civil War is a drama in which technology played a major role.

Railroads
and the Telegraph

In addition to enabling an increase in the production of cotton, technology also played a role in tying parts of the country together economically, socially, and politically. In the 1830s, canals provided the means to transport goods between the Northwest and the Northeast. After 1840, however, railroads increasingly became the most popular form of transportation. Western farmers shipped their products east on the railroads. The same rails delivered manufactured goods to farmers and farming communities in the West. The rate of growth of the railroads demonstrates the nation's increased reliance on this form of transportation. In 1840, the United States had a total of 2,818 miles of railroad track. By 1850, the mileage had increased to 9,021. Construction of new rails exploded during the 1850s. In 1860, there was more than three times the amount of track across America than there had been just a decade earlier. Much of this growth occurred in the Northeast. The region that saw the least amount of railroad construction during the 1850s was the South.

At the start of the Civil War, railroads had already changed American business and transportation by lowering the cost of carrying freight from place to place. A farmer could live far away from the marketplace and still be connected to that marketplace through the railroad. It was less expensive and saved time to transport goods by rail, and a shipper could ship larger amounts of freight on trains than he could by horse and wagon. In addition, railways decreased the amount of travel time. This helped to connect states with one another. As historian John E. Clark Jr. points out, "Railroads traveled faster and farther—all day, every day, and in all kinds of weather—than any other form of transportation then known to mankind." In 1861, the United States was a young nation, but it also was a nation affected by the changing technology in transportation.

The North held a huge advantage in railroads at the beginning of the Civil War. Northern states had more than twice as much track mileage as the states of the Confederacy. To make matters worse, the gauge—the distance between the tracks—was less standardized in the South. Different companies often used different-sized gauges. Although Northern railroads did not all use the same gauge, there was a greater level of gauge consistency than there was in the South. Both sides struggled with this obstacle, but Northern companies worked out many of the problems for themselves. During the war, Southern railroad companies often bickered with Confederate officers. This led to long delays and resulted in less efficient use of the railways.

The North's familiarity with and reliance on railroads led to the Union's extensive use of the rail system throughout the war. As historian John E. Clark Jr. states, "The Civil War was a railroad war." Although the South did not have as many miles of railroads or the capacity to extend its lines, the Confederacy also used the new technology during its struggle against the Union.

Railroads enabled military commanders to move troops, equipment, and supplies over long distances more quickly than

An indispensable tool during the Civil War, the railroad was used to transport soldiers and supplies to reinforce regiments in the battlefield. Cannons were soon built on railcars (above), *eliminating the need to construct and dismantle artillery platforms in the battlefield.*

by marching, which was the traditional means of military transportation. Although marching remained the primary method of moving troops from one location to the next, the use of railways enabled commanders to change the size of armies literally overnight. Commanders used railroads to send reinforcements to the site of a coming battle and sometimes to the fighting during a battle. Historian Archer Jones claims that the use of railroads to send out and organize troops at strategic points has "an almost revolutionary importance."

Equally important, the large armies needed reliable streams of supplies. John E. Clark Jr. maintains, "Iron rails became logistics and communications lifelines. The armies' success or failure depended on the men and materiel provided by their government and carried them by railroads." Railroads served as the pipeline for food, blankets, arms, munitions, letters, and anything else a moving group of tens of thousands of men might need or want. Supply depots allowed the army to send supplies by rail to points near their troops before transporting the materials the remaining distance overland by mule. Military commanders in both the North and South also used railroads to transport wounded and sick soldiers away from the front to receive medical treatment.

Railroads allowed the North to benefit from its industrial advantages. Military trains carried mobile artillery. This allowed commanders to reposition heavy guns for both defensive and offensive purposes. As the war went on, the military began to keep some artillery permanently mounted on railcars. This reduced the preparation time for combat. Railcar artillery pieces were almost always ready to be thrust into battle. This was a marked improvement over the use of horses to haul big guns. Guns that were pulled by horses required artillery platforms that had to be constructed and placed before the guns could engage in battle. With a gun on a railway car, the bed of the car served as the artillery platform. In some cases, the rails allowed the car to absorb the shock of the gun's firing by allowing the car to slide back on the rails. This innovation eliminated the need for the continual reconstruction of a platform each time a military force moved an artillery piece.

In war, an army needs to find ways to provide logistics effectively and efficiently. Logistics involves the getting of supplies and equipment and the transportation of troops and other personnel. Historian Frank E. Vandiver states, "Mass war meant mass logistics." The Civil War was, indeed, a mass war. The demands of such a war required new solutions that had never before been tried. The railroads were a key element in developing strategies to tackle logistical needs. As historian John E. Clark Jr. explains,

> Superior organization and management, as demonstrated by its skillful use of railroads, made a genuine contribution to Union victory. The Confederacy's leaders, in contrast, proved unable to recognize or adapt to the demands of an increasingly logistics-driven conflict. The failure of its war management, as seen in part by its inability to organize the Southern railroads effectively to support the war effort, thus represents an important, if little studied, factor in Confederate defeat.

As military commanders adapted to the needs of war, their skill at doing so had great consequences on the war itself. Field commanders who excelled logistically often fared well in battle. President Abraham Lincoln searched for a Union general who could win battles. He finally found one in General Ulysses S. Grant. General Grant took great pains to make sure that the logistics for his army were handled properly.

Southern general Pierre G.T. Beauregard used the rails to his advantage at the First Battle of Bull Run in July 1861, the first major battle of the war. Initially, Union troops surged forward, and the rebels retreated. Beauregard shifted troops under Joseph E. Johnston from the Shenandoah Valley to Bull Run via the railroad. Johnston's troops arrived at the battlefield at a critical moment and helped the South to turn the tide of battle against the Federals. Archer Jones believes that this use of railroads created a "paranoid Union overestimate of Confederate capacity for strategic troop movements by rail." Jones's analysis may explain why so many of the early Union commanders acted so timidly when they engaged the enemy. Other significant Confederate uses of railroads include the defense

The Importance of Timely Communication

An incident that occurred during the Battle of Malvern Hill, the last battle of the Seven Days Battles, demonstrates the importance of the telegraph during wartime. Confederate forces under General Robert E. Lee were driving McClellan's Army of the Potomac off Virginia's James Peninsula. Lee sent orders to General John B. Magruder, commanding him to take a position directly across from the Union forces in a particular location. After his local guides led Magruder and his men on a long and wandering trek through the rugged terrain, Magruder's force finally reached the line of battle. In the meantime, Lee (who knew nothing about Magruder's delayed arrival) had sent orders to Magruder, directing him to attack the Union position. Although Lee sent the orders early in the day, Magruder did not receive them until much later. Because the orders did not name a specific time for the attack, Magruder had no reason to think that the orders were not up to date. After sending the first set of orders, however, Lee had sent another order to attack.

Magruder assumed that his attack was part of an overall assault on the Union force. A simple telegram exchange between Lee and Magruder could have clarified the situation for both generals. The timeliness of the orders had passed, however, resulting in an uncoordinated and sloppy Confederate attack that ended in failure. Lee's opportunity to deal a deadly blow to the retreating Union army was gone. Lee confronted Magruder and demanded to know why he had attacked. Magruder explained that Lee himself had ordered him to attack—twice! Despite the technological limitations that led to this failure, Lee soon reassigned Magruder to the Western Theater of Operations.

of Chattanooga, Tennessee, in the summer of 1862. General Braxton Bragg transported more than 31,000 soldiers from 250 miles away in Tupelo, Mississippi. Bragg's reinforcements drove the Union force back. Chattanooga was an important rail junction for the South, and Bragg's efforts postponed the fall of the city for another year.

Civilian leaders in the South understood the importance of the railroads to the war effort. Jefferson Davis, the president of the Confederacy, wanted to coordinate an efficient transportation system using the railways. Before the war, Davis was one of the first to argue for a transcontinental railroad. As Confederate president, Davis requested legislation from the Confederate Congress to empower him to seize the railroads in the South to guarantee their assistance. The Confederate Congress passed such a law, but Davis never made use of it. Thus, Davis had the power to organize railroads in the South, but he never used this authority. As a result, the inefficiencies of the Southern railroads helped to limit the success of the Southern cause.

The Union took a decidedly different approach to railroad companies in the North. Although the federal government threatened to seize the railroads, it also offered incentives to rail companies to gain their cooperation. Because it needed efficient, working rail companies to wage the war, the federal government agreed to pay rates at levels that were profitable for the railroad companies. The government also took steps to ensure that military commanders did not impede railroad operations.

Facing a defensive war, the South held the strategic advantage of having interior lines of communication and transportation. The new Confederate government had to try to use a railroad network that included several unrelated systems that did not fit together, however. Different rail companies used different gauges of track. Different rail lines entered some cities, but these rails often remained unconnected. Throughout the war, the Southern rail system suffered from a lack of necessary parts, inadequate maintenance, and no centralized authority to determine the priority of the existing rail lines. As a result, the Confederacy failed to make efficient use of its strategic advantage of interior rail lines. The use of railroad lines did not lessen shortages of food or supplies to either the civilian population or the troops in the field.

The importance of railroads is also evident in the Union strategy. That strategy focused on seizing and holding the cities of Corinth, Mississippi; Chattanooga, Tennessee; and Atlanta, Georgia. All of these cities were critical junctions for railroads in the South. The location of railroads also helped determine battle sites. Clark points out that "Every major battle east of the Mississippi River took place within twenty miles of a railroad or navigable river."

General William T. Sherman certainly understood the value of railroads in waging and winning a war. As his army moved south, Sherman first secured the rail lines to supply his large army. Then, he ordered his men to destroy any rail lines that might benefit the South. Sherman's army famously tore up rail lines, burned the ties, heated the rails, and then made the rails unusable by twisting the hot metal around trees. These twists of rail soon were called "Sherman's neckties." Southerners condemned Sherman's tactics, but his methods destroyed the ability of the South to wage war. The importance of railroads can also be seen in Sherman's Atlanta campaign and in his March to the Sea. Sherman relied on the rails to supply his army as he approached Atlanta. He captured the city on September 2, 1864. Before he abandoned Atlanta and headed toward the Atlantic Ocean, Sherman destroyed as much railroad track as he could. Sherman understood that without the railroad, the Confederacy was incapable of meeting the logistical needs of war.

THE TELEGRAPH

In addition to having an advantage in transportation infrastructure, the North also held an advantage in the area of communications. In 1861, rapid communication over long distances was accomplished by means of the telegraph. The telegraph is a machine that is used to transmit and receive messages over long distances. Typically, the word *telegraph* is used to describe an electrical telegraph system. A message sent and received over the telegraph is called a telegram or cablegram. Such messages also were known as wires or cables, for short.

Although the invention of the telegraph happened before the war, the technology found new uses in wartime. One of the ways in which the Civil War is unique is the way old and new technologies were tangled together. Sometimes this tangling occurred smoothly. In other instances, it led to friction as the forces of tradition and modernity clashed. During the war, military commanders and civilian leaders relied on both primitive means and the most advanced forms of communication. The U.S. Army used a dual approach to achieve effective communication on the battlefield and between commanders and Washington. The military made use of the nation's many miles of telegraph line to send and receive messages quickly. The Army often carried telegraph lines with it. Soldiers strung wires behind the troops as they advanced into enemy territory. The Army also had a Signal Corps, a branch of the military that used flags and torches to send messages.

TELEGRAPH USE BEFORE THE WAR

Joseph Henry was an American scientist and later the first secretary of the Smithsonian Institution. He improved the early telegraph in the late 1820s by adding two important innovations. First, he increased the power of the telegraph's electromagnet by increasing the amount of wire wrapped around the iron core and adding cloth insulation. These improvements made his magnet 100 times more powerful than the ones produced by William Sturgeon, the inventor of the electromagnet. Second, Henry developed the concept of the electrical relay to combat low battery power. Because the wire naturally resisted the electrical signal, Henry needed more battery power to send messages farther. He determined the distance that a current traveled along the wire before it weakened. At that point, Henry placed a small iron key that moved if the current faded. When the key was triggered, it moved. This movement closed a second circuit, which in turn was connected to a second battery. The second battery continued to send the message on with full power. This method of electrical relays was repeated as many times as necessary to send a message over great distances.

Joseph Henry went on to become a professor at Princeton University. A painter-turned-inventor named Samuel Morse took over much of Henry's work. Henry did not patent his telegraph, and he offered his ideas to Morse. Intrigued by the possibilities of the telegraph, Morse took many of Henry's ideas and in 1840 received a patent for the electromagnetic telegraph. Morse did not give credit to Henry for his contributions to the technology.

Although Morse was not a scientist, he made one vital contribution that made the telegraph more useful: the Morse code. Morse established a combination of short and long bursts of electricity that represented different letters of the alphabet. In response to these bursts, a receiver then moved a pencil across a piece of paper. A receiver registered a short burst as a dot and a long burst as a dash. The technology of the telegraph now could be used to transmit information almost instantaneously.

Even though much of the credit for the invention belonged to Joseph Henry, Samuel Morse held the patent for the electromagnetic telegraph. In 1843, Morse won a government contract to construct a telegraph line between Washington, D.C., and Baltimore, Maryland. Forty miles separated the two cities. This offered Morse an excellent opportunity to display the capabilities of his gadget. First, Morse needed to run his line. The Baltimore & Ohio Railroad permitted Morse to use the railroad's right-of-way, thereby eliminating the need for Morse to purchase tracts of land. From this point on, telegraph wires consistently paralleled railroad tracks. Initially, Morse tried to bury his cable, but the insulation on the cable did not offer enough protection to the wire inside. Next, he tried to run the cable above ground, on top of wooden poles. This solution reduced the need to insulate the entire wire. To maintain the current, Morse added glass insulators where the cable touched the pole.

On May 11, 1844, Samuel Morse sent his first message over the 40-mile wire. "Everything worked well," he said, using the trademark dots and dashes of the code that bears his name. Nearly two weeks later, on May 24, Morse publicly showed the capability of his machine as he transmitted the message "What hath God wrought?" between the two cities. News spread, and American communities clamored to be linked with other cities by telegraph. The experiment thrilled the nation, and crews set about laying telegraph lines across the country.

By 1860, the United States had more than 50,000 miles of telegraph wire connecting cities all across the country. In 1861, the year the Civil War began, a telegraph wire connected New York with San Francisco—the first transcontinental telegraph. The effects of the New York-to-San Francisco line were immediate: The famed Pony Express ceased operations just two days later. The technology of communication changed the way Americans sent and received international, national, state, and personal news.

THE TELEGRAPH DURING THE WAR

News of the secession of Southern states from the Union spread across telegraph lines in late 1860 and early 1861. The same lines carried word of the fall of Fort Sumter in April 1861. President Lincoln used the technology when he sent out his call for 75,000 volunteers to put down the rebellion. During the war, America quickly learned ways to use the telegraph. Newspaper reporters submitted their stories via the wire. The telegraph also influenced military operations. According to Charles D. Ross, the telegraph "would dramatically change military command." The technology allowed commanders to gather much-needed intel-

Above, *soldiers string wires to telegraph battery wagons. The telegraph and Morse code were used heavily during the Civil War, both in military and civilian activities. The telegraph enabled regiments to update regional command centers and government officials in Washington, D.C. Military telegraph systems also benefited newspapers, whose journalists were able to instantaneously transmit their stories to their editors.*

ligence and reposition their troops from a centralized command post. The telegraph also allowed civilian authorities to keep track of generals and receive regular updates from the front.

When Fort Sumter fell, Secretary of War Simon Cameron took steps to gain control of telegraph and railroad lines in the North. Technically, the telegraph remained in private hands. In practice, however, the vice president of the Pennsylvania Railroad, Thomas A. Scott, took control of the telegraphs, centralizing all operations. Scott established a telegraph office in Washington, D.C., in the War Department building. The American Telegraph Company connected its lines to the War Department and other key military sites in the capital, enabling the federal government to have access to the rest of the North. The executive mansion (the White House) did not receive a telegraph office, however. Because of this, President Lincoln became a common figure in the office of the War Department, where he went to send and receive telegrams.

One issue facing both sides was that cable lines still operated between the North and the South. People on both sides could easily listen in on the cable chatter of those on the other side. Because of this, on April 21, 1861, the American Telegraph Company did something extraordinary. The company divided into two divisions, one for the North, and the other for the South. The two divisions then cut the lines between the two national capitals, Richmond, Virginia, and Washington, D.C. Throughout the conflict, two branches of the same telegraph company worked cooperatively with competing governments engaged in war.

The first meaningful use of the telegraph to carry out tactics on the battlefield occurred in December 1862, at Fredericksburg, Virginia. The Union line was spread out, and the central command was unable to see the whole battlefield. Union telegraph lines linked each flank of the army with the command center. Although Union commanders bungled the battle plan and lost the battle, the telegraph proved its tactical value.

CONFEDERATE TELEGRAPHY

In the spring of 1861, the Confederate Congress passed a bill empowering President Jefferson Davis to seize control of all telegraph lines within the Confederacy. The Southern head of the American Telegraph Company (called the Southern Telegraph Company during the war), William S. Morris, kept a good working relationship with the government of the Confederate States of America (CSA), thus preventing any government takeover of the lines. Morris kept telegraph lines open and usable by Confederate authorities until the closing days of the conflict. Morris even managed to pay dividends to company shareholders until early 1865. The result was that the Confederate government never took control of the telegraph lines in the South. When Confederate general Braxton Bragg tried to seize telegraph lines in 1862, Confederate government officials ordered him to hand over control to the company.

SECURITY

The use of the telegraph also led to increased espionage activities: spying. Almost anyone could listen in on the telegraph lines. All that was needed was a telegraph key. Before the war, employees of telegraph companies had small, pocket-sized telegraph keys that they used to test the reliability of cables. During the war, spies used these same keys to tap into the lines and gain valuable enemy information. Sometimes, telegraphers loyal to one side sent false messages over the enemy's wires.

To combat enemy attempts to intercept information sent by telegraph, both sides eventually sent their messages encoded or enciphered. In a coded message, the content of the message is converted into another form to limit the number of people who can understand the message. In order to be effective, the receiver of the coded message must be able to decode it—to reverse the process so that the words return to their original meaning. The Civil War was the first war in which electrically transmitted messages were encoded. Generally, during the war, the Union had the most advanced forms of cryptography

Telegraph operators working in the battlefield were often vulnerable to gunfire and shelling, but continued to transmit and receive encrypted messages. Above, a telegraph battery wagon in Virginia.

(writing in secret code). The Union used a machine called a route cipher.

The telegraph also allowed the federal government to restrict the flow of information—a form of censorship. Secretary of War Simon Cameron instructed the civilian telegraph operators to screen messages for content. Information that was judged harmful to the Union cause was sent to a member of the president's cabinet for approval. Screeners sent coded messages to the appropriate office or examined them to determine their legitimacy. No government official ever informed reporters that someone censored their telegraphs.

The telegraph played a part in telling the story of war from the field. At the First Battle of Bull Run, the first significant engagement of the war, newspaper reporters sent updates from the field. Initial reports were favorable to the North, as the Union soldiers pushed the rebels back. As the day wore on, however, the Southern force pushed back and defeated the Federals. The conflicting reports from the battlefield confused many Northerners. Army officials saw the need for a calmer approach to sending news over the wire. After the loss at Bull Run, the newly appointed general of the Army of the Potomac, George B. McClellan, met with reporters to discuss voluntary censorship of news cables. On August 2, 1861, reporters agreed to withhold any information that could help the Confederacy.

THE SIGNAL CORPS

The idea for a signal service came from an unlikely source: an Army doctor serving in Texas. Albert James Myer introduced the idea in 1856. Myer believed that a specially trained signal service could benefit the U.S. military. He recommended using a system of aerial telegraphy in which corps members communicated with one another using flags during the day and torches at night. The Army put Myer's system into operation on June 21, 1860, less than a year before the outbreak of the Civil War. Initially, Myer was the only signal officer in the U.S. Army Signal Corps.

The Army first put Myer and his system into use out West, during the Navajo expedition of 1860–1861. Myer also signaled during a June 1861 military engagement at Fort Monroe in Hampton, Virginia. Myer's system worked well and helped the

Union commanders to remain in communication with their officers. Despite these successes, Myer encountered staffing problems. The Army periodically ordered officers and enlisted men to assist Myer, but the military units retained command of the men. When the units ordered trained operators to other posts, Myer's operations suffered from a lack of consistency. To deal with this problem, on March 3, 1863, the Army formed the U.S. Army Signal Corps. Despite Myer's belief in the necessity and value of visual signals, the telegraph soon became the communication method of choice for most commanders. The Signal Corps's responsibilities increased after the war, however, when the Signal Corps took over the telegraph (1867) and, for a time, weather observations. Although the technology used by the Signal Corps has changed, Myer's vision of a military unit entrusted with battlefield communications lives on today.

Weapons of Death

I n the 50 years before the Civil War, the world saw a rapid rise in technological advances. Inventions that modern America takes for granted were in their infancy. Many of these creations improved the quality of life; others, however, were designed to end life. The Civil War presented military planners with the opportunity to try new weapons as part of their overall strategy. As these new technologies were put into use, the war presented new challenges that sometimes required the development of additional new technologies. The role of technology in waging war is seen clearly in the development of artillery and firearms.

ARTILLERY

Any firearms larger than small arms, which include handguns, muskets, and rifles, are called cannon or artillery. Cannons come in all shapes and sizes and are categorized as either smoothbore or rifled. Additional distinctions relate to the weight, in pounds, of the fired projectile; the size of a barrel's bore diameter, or caliber; the method of loading (muzzle or breech); and the trajectory, or flight arc, of the projectiles. The short-barreled cannons called mortars had a high trajectory, and the long-barreled cannons called guns had a flat trajectory. The trajectory of a howitzer—a cannon with a barrel longer than that of a mortar but shorter than that of a gun—was in between that of a mortar and a gun.

Often, cannons were named after their inventors or after the factory that produced them. Examples include Dahlgren, Napoleon, Parrott, and Whitworth. Civil War cannons were made of bronze, iron, or steel. Both sides favored the Napoleon, a muzzle-loaded, smoothbore, 12-pound gun-howitzer. The Napoleon was named after Louis Napoleon—Emperor Napoleon III of France—who directed its development. The United States added the Napoleon to its arsenal four years before the start of the war. A versatile gun, the Napoleon was used both to attack and to defend positions. Effective up to 1,700 yards (1,554 meters), the Napoleon's range extended another 800 yards (732 meters). This smoothbore cannon was capable of firing canister shot (described later in this chapter) with deadly precision. Additionally, the weapon was comparatively light and easy to transport. This made it a popular component in artillery units.

The 10-pound Parrott was the most commonly used rifled artillery piece in the war. The Parrott could fire a projectile about 2,300 yards (2,100 meters) and packed a powerful punch against defensive works. The Union used rifled cannon such as the Parrot in the sieges of Vicksburg in 1863 and Atlanta in 1864. In order to fire accurately, however, gunners needed to spot their target visually. This limited the effective range of rifled cannon. Consequently, the shorter-ranged, smoothbore Napoleons provided sufficient accuracy for most Civil War artillery units.

Sizes of guns ranged from the small and easily portable howitzers (8-inch and 10-inch) to the large, heavy guns on naval ships. Both sides fired solid shot, or exploding shells, and chain shot. Chain shot consisted of two solid balls joined by a chain. Gunners aimed the chain shot at the masts of enemy warships, in the hope of disabling the ships. Artillery technology pointed the way to the warfare of the future, but it did not keep up with the technology of firearms. Because most breech-loaded cannons were undependable and more difficult to maneuver than muzzle-loaded cannons, almost all Civil War cannons were muzzle loaded.

FIREARMS

In 1861, smoothbore muskets served as the foundation of military tactics for the infantry, the Army's foot soldiers. The smoothbore musket was a firearm with shortcomings that influenced tactics. Smoothbores had questionable accuracy and a limited range. Generally, bullets fired from smoothbores could do little damage beyond a hundred yards. The range for accuracy for these weapons was even less. Because of these shortcomings, military commanders gathered their troops together for large assaults on defensive positions. If enough men in the attacking force reached the defenders, the attackers could overwhelm the enemy in hand-to-hand fighting by their numbers alone. As this example shows, offensive tactics relied on brute strength and force of numbers and were not helped by the inaccuracy of the standard firearms.

All of this changed with the introduction and adoption of rifled muskets. Loading through the muzzle was the standard for early rifles, as it was for the smoothbores, and the increased accuracy and range of these new firearms killed a large number of attacking soldiers. Rifle range extended the killing zone of small arms from 100 yards to about half a mile, or 880 yards. Large-scale frontal assaults against entrenched defenders armed with rifles became both impractical and highly dangerous. Commanders often failed to recognize this new reality of war, however. Soldiers in the Civil War fought with rifles, but many

Newly developed cannons projected larger cannonballs more effectively than ever before. Rifled cannons caused ammunition to spin as it was shot out of the barrel, which improved the accuracy and distance of the weapon. Above, rifled cannons in the Arsenal Yard in Charleston, South Carolina.

of their commanders still used the tactics of smoothbores. This led to failed assaults and high casualties in many battles.

Similar developments took place in artillery weapons. Smoothbore cannon had a range of about one mile (1,609 meters). When rifling was added to artillery pieces, it increased their range. Many of the advances in artillery came in the kinds of shells the big guns fired, however. Rifled cannons had at least two distinct advantages over smoothbores: First, the rifled cannon could fire projectiles in a flat trajectory. Second, the same artillery pieces could fire on enemy targets from greater distances and deliver more firepower. Because smoothbore

Faking Technology

The technology in artillery changed some tactics and affected the outcome of battles. Sometimes, however, commanders used the appearance of technology to deceive the enemy. One of the best-known instances of this sort of trick occurred during the 1862 Peninsular Campaign. Confederate general Joseph E. Johnston shaped logs to look like cannons, painted them black, and set them up in place of real cannons in his defenses near Centerville, Virginia. From a distance, the Union troops could not tell the difference. Union general George McClellan lingered, fearing to advance against such a powerful defensive position. The trick worked. It allowed Johnston and his men to retreat across the Rappahannock River. The so-called Quaker guns gave the false impression of technological strength.

Johnston was not the only commander to use Quaker guns. Other Confederate commanders used the same technique. Union officers also employed logs masquerading as cannon to disguise retreats or other troop movements. Quaker guns proved to be an effective deterrent that allowed a force to withdraw unimpeded. As historian Maurice D'Aoustand writes, "Strategically placed, these bogus batteries could effectively transform a thinly defended line into one that was bristling with cannon muzzles, and they were often instrumental in thwarting the enemy." Thus, not all technology was new—or even real. Some of it was simply old-fashioned trickery designed to mimic the power of real technology.

cannons remained effective in disrupting infantry charges, however, there was little need and no rush to convert to rifled cannons. Additionally, much of the fighting took place in wooded and hilly terrain, and smoothbore cannons performed well in those environments.

Defensive preparations offered some protection against Napoleons. This preparation forced attacking gunners to use other weapons to dislodge defenders. Breastworks—temporary fortifications made of earth, wood, or anything that provided cover—limited the effectiveness of artillery guns, because fieldworks made of earth absorbed much of the shock of the explosion. Howitzers overcame this defensive obstacle by increasing the angle at which the fired shell left the barrel and descended. A howitzer usually features a short barrel. An artillery gun fires shells at a relatively flat trajectory, but a howitzer fires shells at steep trajectories. A short-barreled mortar fires shells at an even greater trajectory. Howitzers offered the advantage of firing over defensive works and directly into the heart of the enemy camp.

GRAPE AND CANISTER SHOT

Several kinds of ammunition were fired from cannons during the Civil War. Two of these were intended for use against enemy troops: grapeshot and canister shot. Grapeshot was a collection of solid-shot balls wrapped in canvas or some other cloth and tied shut with a string. The term *grapeshot* came about from the fact that the ammunition pack looked like a cluster of grapes. When grapeshot was fired, the shock of the blast disintegrated the cloth wrapping and dispersed the shot in a scattered pattern along its trajectory. Such a projectile was a deadly weapon against infantry.

Canister shot was another kind of antipersonnel ammunition fired from cannons. Similar to grapeshot, canister shot is a kind of cannon version of a shotgun blast, in which loosely packed slugs are fired from an artillery gun. This type of shot was designed to disrupt advancing enemy troops by releasing a large number of balls at one time from each cannon. Canister shot usually was fired into a group of soldiers. A single round of canister shot was made up of a round, metal container filled with iron or lead balls. Packed in sawdust, the balls quickly scattered when a cannon fired the canister. If balls were in short supply, scrap metal, nails, wire, or anything made out of metal replaced the round shot. Generally, the cylindrical canister was made of tin. The ends were plugged with disks made of metal or wood. For larger cannons, the canister was made of iron. The entire can was usually coated with beeswax to waterproof it. A cartridge bag made of cloth and filled with gunpowder was fastened to one end of the canister. The gunpowder in the bag served as the charge that launched the round from the cannon.

A fired canister fragmented, spreading shrapnel and releasing the metal balls within it to clear a cone-shaped area with the blast. Within 250 yards, canister shot was an effective and deadly tool against enemy troops. A mass of infantry was no match for the destructive firepower of canister shot. During the Civil War, some artillery commanders used a technique in which cannons were aimed at the ground in front of advancing enemy troops. The exploded canisters struck the ground, and balls ricocheted off the ground, expanding the target area. Union artillery effectively used this technique at the Battle of Gettysburg against the Confederate troops who were attempting to take Seminary Ridge. Throughout the war, artillery units preferred canister shot to grapeshot, believing canister shot to be more effective.

THE LAND MINE

Confederate troops improvised one of their weapons and, by doing so, created a new use for shells. On May 4, 1862, Union cavalry advancing on a road near Yorktown, Virginia, detonated an underground shell, or land mine. The retreating Southern troops had buried shells in the ground, with strings attached to the shells' fuses. The ends of the strings were placed above ground. When such a string was pulled or tripped, it activated the fuse and detonated the shell. Union troops expressed outrage over the practice, which they considered barbaric. General George McClellan threatened to force Southern prisoners to clear land mines to protect his men.

The use of land mines did not become widespread during the Civil War. The conflict's most memorable use of a land mine occurred during the Siege of Petersburg, a strategically important city south of Richmond. When the two armies became bogged down in a stalemate that lasted for months, a Union officer made an unusual suggestion. Lieutenant Colonel Henry Pleasants recommended digging a mine shaft underneath the enemy's defensive lines and packing the shaft with explosives. Pleasants believed that the explosion would kill enemy soldiers and open a hole in the defensive line.

By late June 1864, digging was underway. On July 17, Pleasants determined that the shaft was directly under the Confederate line. To complete their preparations, workers created a T by digging out a chamber 38 feet (11.6 meters) in one direction and 37 (11.3 meters) feet in the other, at a right angle to the main shaft. Southerners guessed that the Federals were attempting to mine underneath their defensive lines, but their efforts to find and cut into the Union tunnel's main shaft failed.

The Federals placed about 8,000 pounds (3,826 kilograms) of gunpowder, packed in 320 kegs, 22 feet (6.7 meters) beneath the Confederate line. Union soldiers then blocked the main entrance to the shaft to concentrate the force of the blast under the enemy's defensive positions. On the morning of July 30, 1864, the fuse detonated the explosion. Historian Charles D. Ross describes the scene:

> The ground began to rumble. For a brief instant the ground
> beneath the Confederate lines became rounded like a

giant bubble and then it exploded. Flame and smoke blew out of the ground, lifting up with it men and artillery and wagons and massive pieces of earth. The column reached hundreds of feet in the air, spreading out like a mushroom and raining down guns, stones, dirt, and human limbs all around.

The explosion blew a hole in the ground that measured nearly 200 feet long (61 meters); 60 to 80 feet (18–24 meters) wide; and 30 feet (9 meters) deep. This huge crater was where the Confederate defensive line had been just moments earlier. The crater is still visible today.

THE COAL TORPEDO

Another innovation conceived and carried out by Confederate operatives was known as the coal torpedo. In the Civil War, the word *torpedo* was used to describe many kinds of explosive devices. Captain Thomas Edgeworth Courtenay, a member of the Confederate Secret Service, invented a weapon that he labeled the coal shell. Most people called it the coal torpedo. Coal torpedoes were small, hollow iron castings that were made to look like pieces of coal. Explosives or gunpowder was packed inside each casting. A threaded plug closed the opening, and beeswax waterproofed the entire shell. To complete its disguise, each torpedo was coated in coal dust. Operatives placed the coal torpedoes in coal supplies intended for Union steamships. These ships burned coal to produce the steam that drove them. Courtenay hoped that workers would shovel the coal torpedoes into the ship's firebox, which would lead to an explosion.

Coal torpedoes weighed approximately 3 to 4 pounds (1.3 to 1.8 kilograms). Each shell was irregularly sized to mimic coal but was about 4 inches (10.2 centimeters) on each side. A coal torpedo packed an explosive punch comparable to that of a 6-pound shrapnel shell. (A shrapnel shell is a four-inch hollow

After several months of patiently waiting outside Petersburg, Virginia (above), Union forces excavated a large T-shaped tunnel under enemy lines and packed it with almost 8,000 pounds of gunpowder. The Union set off the explosive, blasting open a large gap in Confederate defenses, as well as an enormous hole in the ground.

cannonball filled with gunpowder and 24 musket balls.) A single coal torpedo was too small to sink a steamboat. The shell could cause a secondary explosion if it did enough damage to the ship's boiler, however. Boiler explosions were not unheard of, and such an explosion usually destroyed a ship. The successful detonation of a coal torpedo on a steamship could sink the ship and hide all evidence of sabotage. Historians believe that coal torpedoes sank several Union steamers.

HAND GRENADES

Another technology used in the Civil War was a small hand-thrown bomb called a grenade. William F. Ketchum received a patent for this deadly invention on August 20, 1861. The Union army used the weapon in some sieges, including those at Vicksburg and, later, Petersburg. The grenade included an explosive charge that was packed into the nose and a percussion cap in the tip. To increase the chances that the bomb would land on the percussion cap, cardboard fins were added to a wooden rod that projected from the back of the device. The resulting projectile resembled a large dart. With the cap located at the bottom of the shell, the grenade had to be thrown in a high arc to detonate. This was not always possible. Ketchum grenades came in one-, three-, five-, and six-pound sizes. The Confederates responded with their own grenade, called the Raines grenade.

Despite the small bombs' possibilities, the Union troops who used the Ketchum grenades found that the hand-thrown explosives were not reliable. If a grenade failed to land on its cap, the explosive did not detonate. This made it possible for an enemy soldier to pick up the unexploded shell and fling it back at the Union troops. The Confederate version, the Raines, did not perform any better. The technology simply did not yet match the idea for a grenade.

Authors Thomas Dickey and Peter George report a story that describes the use of Ketchum hand grenades during the Battle of Port Hudson from the Confederate point of view. The authors quote the following account by Confederate lieutenant Howard C. Wright:

> The enemy had come this time prepared with hand grenades to throw into our works from the outside. When these novel missiles commenced falling among the Arkansas troops they did not know what to make of them, and the first few which they caught not having burst, they threw them back upon the enemy in the ditch. This time

many of them exploded and their character was at once revealed to our men. Always equal to any emergency, they quickly devised a scheme. . . . Spreading blankets behind the parapet, the grenades fell harmlessly into them, where-upon our boys would pick them up and hurling them with much greater force down the moat they would almost in-variably explode.

The limitations of these early grenades did not deter others from improving on the designs. Grenades are now a staple weapon of war. They come in a variety of models for different purposes, not all of which are designed to be deadly.

TECHNOLOGY AND SMALL ARMS

Technology played a role in the way men and armies fought the Civil War. Perhaps nowhere else is technology's presence more evident than in small arms—handheld firearms such as pistols. Author James Biser Whisker identifies six innovations in technology that occurred after the War of 1812. Each of these had a deep impact on the Civil War. These innovations are the percussion cap, the minié ball, the cylindro-conoidal bullet, ri-fling, the breech-loading rifle, and the production of rifles using fully interchangeable parts. Each of these innovations occurred either before or during the Civil War. Whisker maintains that "the advances that firearms technology had made in the fifty years following the War of 1812 seemed to be greater than had been made in the hundreds of years since the introduction of hand cannons until the beginning of the nineteenth century."

THE PERCUSSION CAP

First introduced around 1830, the percussion cap made it possi-ble to fire muzzle-loaders under any weather conditions. Before this invention, firearms relied on a device called a flintlock to ignite the powder and discharge the shot. Although the flintlock itself was an improvement on earlier ways to discharge firearms, it had a major shortcoming. Flintlocks were undependable in wet conditions. Flintlocks also were likely to misfire, even under better conditions. The British army conducted tests to determine whether to adopt the percussion caps. The British tests of flintlock firearms revealed that the weapons misfired more than 400 times out of 1,000. In contrast, shots fired by percussion caps misfired only 4.5 times out of 1,000. Additionally, it was possible to load the percussion caps more quickly, thus increasing the rate of firing.

A percussion cap is a small copper or brass cylinder. The cylinder has one closed end and one open end. In the base, at the closed end, is a small amount of a substance called fulminate of mercury, which is highly sensitive to shock and friction. This makes fulminate of mercury ideal as a primary explosive to be used in triggering. To fire the percussion cap, it is placed at the rear of the gun barrel, over a hollow metal dimple. When the gun's trigger is pulled, a hammer strikes the percussion cap. This ignites the mercury fulminate. The small explosion sends a flame through the hollow dimple to detonate the main powder charge. The metal casing of the percussion cap helps to protect the initial charge from elements such as water and dampness and increases its reliability.

Pistols required smaller caps than larger firearms such as rifles. Battlefield conditions that called for such actions as shooting while riding a horse or refiring rapidly increased the difficulty of changing the caps. Later modifications, some of which were used during the Civil War, automatically set a new percussion cap into place after each shot. This allowed for faster reloading and discharge of the firearm. Such modifications involved cocking the hammer to move the next cap into place for firing.

In the decade before the Civil War, another improvement eventually made percussion caps obsolete. Ammunition manufacturers combined the primer, the charge, and the bullet into a single metal cartridge. By 1870, breech-loading metal cartridges had replaced the percussion cap technique.

THE MINIÉ BALL

A captain in the French army named Claude Minié forever changed the face of combat. Minié helped to develop a new bullet. Rifles usually were loaded through the muzzle, the end of the barrel. The minié ball was a cone-shaped bullet made of soft lead. To work, the bullet had to be slightly larger than the barrel's bore—the diameter of the hole that extends the length of the barrel. A Civil War soldier loaded a paper cartridge of gunpowder and a bullet into the muzzle and down the barrel of his gun. The paper cartridge offered several advantages over older muzzle-loading techniques in which the gunpowder and the shot were added separately. First, each paper cartridge included a premeasured amount of powder. This limited the number of misfires. Second, the use of cartridges enabled a soldier to fire the gun more rapidly because there was no need to measure the powder. Finally, each paper cartridge was greased with beeswax, tallow (cow fat), or lard (pig fat). These substances helped to keep the powder dry and useable. The greased paper also lubricated the whole package, making it easier for the soldier to load the powder and bullet. The soldier pushed the bullet and powder all the way down the barrel with a ramrod.

Minié's version of the bullet had four grooves on the outside, each filled with grease. The bullet had a cone-shaped hollow space at its base, which included a small iron plug. When the gun was fired, the iron plug drove the softer lead bullet out of the barrel. The force of the blast also drove the iron plug into the lead bullet, which also expanded under the pressure of the blast. The lead expanded as the bullet moved through the barrel, gripping the rifle grooves. The grooves spun the bullet. This spinning action boosted accuracy and increased the velocity and range of the projectile.

Minié invented his famous bullet in 1847. Two years later, he introduced the so-called minié rifle. In contrast to earlier firearms that featured smooth bores, Minié's gun was rifled: It had spiral grooves in the bore. Use of the minié ball and the minié rifle caused horrific injuries on the battlefield. There were thousands of these weapons in the hands of soldiers. The use of these weapons led to more battle wounds and more severe wounds than were seen before the Civil War. The lead bullets often splintered bones; this usually led to fatal infections. Working before the discovery of modern antibiotics, surgeons were forced to amputate the shattered limbs of wounded soldiers to prevent infections.

Use of the bullet in the American Civil War resulted in the widespread adoption of the rifle as a battlefield weapon. The rifle enabled soldiers in defensive positions to inflict high casualties on assaulting troops. This forced a change in offensive and defensive tactics. The minié ball and rifle made most existing battlefield tactics obsolete. The minié ball boasted a large caliber, or diameter: between 13 and 18 millimeters (.51 and .7 inches). This large size accounted for the horrific battlefield injuries. After 1862, many soldiers on both sides carried and used rifled muskets.

BREECHLOADERS

The introduction of rifling increased the time needed to load muzzle-loading weapons, but the introduction of percussion caps and the invention of metal cartridges combined the initial charge, the propellant charge, and the shell—all necessary components to discharge a firearm—into convenient packages. These and other technological advances created the need for a more rapid reloading system. The breechloader offered a solution to this need. Whisker believes that, ultimately, the introduction and adoption of the breech-loading rifle "changed firearms and consequently the nature of warfare."

In a breech-loading rifle, the bullet is loaded at the rear of the barrel, at an opening called the breech. Until the nineteenth century, most firearms used the muzzle-loading system, in which the shell is loaded through the muzzle. The adoption of rifling grooves in barrels made muzzle loading more difficult, however, as it increased reloading time. Breech loading also decreased the amount of time needed to reload because the shell did not have to pass down the entire barrel during the loading process. The advantages in breech loading extended to large cannons. The efficiency of breech loading and the elimination of the long and highly visible ramrod enabled an artillery crew to load its gun out of sight of enemy fire.

Shortly after the adoption of breechloaders, gun manufacturers introduced magazines that held several cartridges. This invention enabled a weapon to fire repeatedly. Rifles with such magazines are called repeating rifles. A repeating rifle has a single barrel that contains several rounds of ammunition. Rounds are loaded into the firing chamber of the barrel, either manually or automatically. Usually, the action of reloading the weapon also resets the firing mechanism for the next shot. Repeating rifles in the Civil War relied on manual action to reload the weapon. Improvements made after the war included automatic reloading, or self-loading rifles.

Single-shot, breech-loaded rifles outperformed muzzle-loaded weapons by decreasing reloading time. Repeating rifles offered an even greater advantage by increasing firepower. Because both sides in the Civil War lacked ammunition supplies, the breech-loading rifle created additional supply problems for those who handled logistics. The North held a decided advantage over the South in its capability to produce weapons and ammunition. The North also had a better transportation infrastructure to keep its armies well supplied.

SHARPSHOOTERS

The introduction of rifled barrels and breech-loaded weapons led to another development in the Civil War: the use of sharpshooters. Many people considered sharpshooting, or sniping, to be beneath the dignity of a civilized society. The harsh conditions of war soon removed that stigma. Almost immediately, sharpshooters became important members of every Union army in the Eastern Theater of Operations. The psychological impact on the Confederate troops was powerful. No longer was it safe for a soldier to expose himself to the enemy, even at a distance of several hundred yards. Sharpshooters changed war for the soldier on the line.

The 1st and 2nd United States Volunteer Sharpshooter Regiments or USSS (U.S. Sharps Shooters) became the best-known sharpshooter units of the war. Hiram Berdan, reportedly the most accurate amateur shooter of his day, formed and trained the USSS. Qualifying recruits had to fire from 200 yards (183 meters) and place 10 consecutive shots within a 10-inch (25-centimeter) bulls-eye. Unlike other Northern units, Berdan's men came from all across the Union. Although some Federal sharpshooters used their own weapons or other preferred gun, most usually carried Sharps rifles, breechloaders designed by a man named Christian Sharps. The success of these men in the field led to the term *sharpshooter*, an adaptation of "Sharps shooters." Confederate sharpshooters usually carried British-made Whitworth rifles, earning them the nickname Whitworth's sharpshooters.

Well equipped and superbly trained, these units served as scouts at the front of advancing columns. Union sharpshooters wore green uniforms and nonreflective hard rubber buttons made by Charles Goodyear. Sharpshooters usually were the first to engage the enemy, acting as skirmishers rather than as snipers. Commanders usually tried to minimize the losses to this group of specially trained soldiers. Thus, sharpshooters performed scout and skirmishing duties but rarely participated in the large-scale assaults of defensive positions in which casualty rates usually were high.

The Confederates formed their own unit of sharpshooters in 1862. Over time, both sides eventually found that regiments

The Civil War was the first time sharpshooters were used in battles. Although they were initially thought to be dishonorable, their effectiveness soon outweighed any moral principles the military command had against using them. A company of sharpshooters accompanied a regiment in battles during the Civil War, and their fatal accuracy was physically and psychologically damaging to the enemy. Above, a sharpshooter named Captain Schwartz, of the 39th New York Regiment.

of sharpshooters were too large to use effectively. Instead, sharpshooters were organized into companies. Commanders assigned these specialized companies to regiments, to serve at the will of the field general. This allowed battlefield commanders to make the best use of their sharpshooters. Commanders usually protected their sharpshooter companies by relieving them of all picket (guard) duty as well as by holding them in reserve during frontal assaults.

MACHINE GUNS

The Gatling gun was best-known repeating firearm of the Civil War era. Dr. Richard J. Gatling, an American inventor, devised the gun in 1861. Gatling received a patent for the weapon the next year. This weapon featured multiple firing pins and breeches connected to several rotating barrels. Each barrel loaded a single round and fired it when the barrel reached a certain spot in the rotation. As the rotation continued, the spent cartridge was ejected and a new round was loaded in it place.

The Gatling gun used multiple rotating barrels powered by a hand crank. The gun fired loose metal cartridge ammunition shells which were fed into the breech by the force of gravity. With its reduced reloading times, the Gatling gun could fire 150 rounds per minute. In addition, because of its multiple barrels, the Gatling gun offered the distinct advantage of loading and firing simultaneously. As some barrels fired their cartridges, the barrels that were being loaded had time to cool down. Because of this, the weapon was not likely to overheat and jam. This allowed the operator to continue firing the weapon. Continuous firing increased the number of rounds that could be fired per minute, increasing firepower.

Because the Gatling gun could fire continuously, many view it as the first machine gun. The weapon did not reload on its own power, however; it depended instead on a hand crank. Improvements were made. Shortly after the Civil War, energy from the firing shots helped to rotate the barrels. Later, electric motors powered the rotation. During the Civil War, Union armies used Gatling's weapon on a limited basis, mostly on gunboats. The weapon proved to be effective, and the basic concept of the gun is still used today.

Ironclads

At the outbreak of the Civil War, the Union developed a strategy to win the conflict. The commanding general of the U.S. Army formulated the idea of establishing a blockade of all Southern ports. Through the so-called Anaconda Plan, the Union determined to seize control of the Mississippi River to cut the South in two. The strengthening grip of the blockade, on the river and against the South's seaports, would cripple the Confederate economy. President Abraham Lincoln liked the plan. Lincoln put the strategy into place through executive order in May 1861, when he ordered the blockade of all Southern ports. Offenders risked losing their cargoes and ships to patrolling Union warships. Although the blockade failed to end all maritime trade in the South, it did hinder much of the local port-to-port trade by the end of the year. The inability of the South to export its cotton wrecked the Southern economy.

To combat the blockade, Southerners turned to their primary international trading partner, Great Britain. Private British citizens invested in blockade-runners—small, sleek boats capable of outrunning warships. These blockade-runners brought weapons and luxury items into Southern ports and sailed away with tobacco and cotton. As the war dragged on, Federal warships became more effective at catching blockade-runners. At the same time, Northern armies advanced into the Confederacy to damage or destroy industries, population centers, and farms. The blockade limited the supply of needed goods and further damaged the Southern economy by preventing the South from selling its dwindling supply of cash crops to foreign buyers. Confederate leaders realized that they needed some way to break the blockade. The blockade's effectiveness meant that the South had to do something different. It was time to search for a technological solution.

A NEW KIND OF WARSHIP

Some military planners decided to try a new kind of warship: an ironclad. An ironclad was a ship powered by a steam engine. Such ships were made of wood but were fitted with iron or steel armor plates. This plating earned them the nickname "ironclads." Ironclads were not new in 1860. Navies around the world had been developing them for more than 20 years. The first battle between ironclads occurred during the U.S. Civil War, however.

Historian Richard Hill explains that ironclads "had three chief characteristics: a metal-skinned hull, steam propulsion, and a main armament of guns capable of firing explosive shells." Hill also maintains that it is "only when all three characteristics are present that a fighting ship can properly be called an ironclad."

Before ironclads, navies usually consisted largely of ships called ships of the line and/or frigates. A ship of the line was a warship with a design that reflected naval tactics developed during more than two centuries, beginning in the seventeenth century. Navies used a line of battle, in which two columns of rival warships passed by each other. As the lines passed, the

By the time the Civil War began, the British and French navies had already con-structed several ironclads—wooden steamships protected by plates of iron or steel—for military use. Described as an "impregnable battery," the ironclad was designed to withstand attacks of explosive artillery that would destroy older, unpro-tected wooden ships. Above, the USS St. Louis, one of the first ironclads constructed by the Union.

ships of each line fired as much artillery as possible at the battle line of the enemy. Larger ships and larger guns consistently led to victory. Navies tried to build their warships as large as pos-sible, all the while increasing the number and size of the guns that the ships carried.

A frigate usually was as long as a ship of the line, but a frig-ate carried lighter guns. Because of their lighter weight, frigates were much faster and often were used as escort vessels or for patrolling purposes. Both ships of the line and frigates were wooden warships that relied on sails for propulsion.

In the nineteenth century, technology changed warships. The first key development in warship design was the addition of effective steam power for propulsion. The first steamships were developed in the second half of the eighteenth century. Typically, early steamboats used paddle wheels to move through the water. Paddle wheels did not meet the needs of warships, however, so naval vessels continued to rely on sails for propulsion. The introduction of the screw propeller in the 1840s convinced navies to accept steam power for their warships. France and Britain expanded the use of steam-powered vessels in their navies throughout the 1840s and 1850s. Steam offered two distinct advantages over the sail power of traditional warships. First, steamboats did not need favorable winds to travel. Second, steamboats could travel at faster and steadier speeds than ships with masts and sails. These improvements offered clear advantages in battle. Wooden ships of the line powered by steam enjoyed a short-lived supremacy on the high seas.

As wooden steamships of the line appeared, however, advances in artillery shells also influenced the technology of warships. The size of a gun was determined by the size and weight of the shell it fired. This meant that an 18-pound gun fired shells that weighed 18 pounds. As naval guns increased in size from 18-pounders to 32-, 36-, and 42-pounders during the 1820s and 1830s, however, wooden ships no longer could withstand their pounding. Some steamships of the line even boasted 68-pound guns.

At nearly the same time, the French developed guns that were capable of firing explosive shells. Other navies quickly adopted such guns. A shot is a large solid projectile fired out of an artillery gun. A shell contains an explosive that either is set on a time-delay fuse or detonates on impact. Explosive shells date back at least to the sixteenth century. Although explosive shells were effective, their use was limited by technology that permitted such shells to be fired only from high trajectory artillery guns. The technology changed in 1823, however, when Frenchman Henri-Joseph Paixhans developed a gun that was capable of firing explosive shells on a flat trajectory. By the 1840s, many navies featured these guns. Although these same navies still had and relied on wooden ships, explosive shells made them all but obsolete.

Explosive shells were capable of shattering wooden hulls. Thus, changes in technology demanded a change in tactics and the development of other new technologies. No longer did it make sense for navies to form lines of battle because explosive shells would likely cause extensive damage to any ships engaged in a battle-line battle. The use of explosive shells also led to the development of armor for ships. To counteract advances in artillery shells, naval planners resorted to metal armor.

In the decade before the Civil War, Britain and France used iron-armored floating batteries—groupings of guns—to increase the effectiveness of their wooden steamships. These floating batteries helped to shell enemy fortifications on shore. Their armor offered some protection against enemy fire. The one drawback to the armored floating batteries was their relative lack of speed. Although they were powered by steam, these batteries were slow and cumbersome. To make use of them, the British and French towed them into position next to their wooden steamships.

When the U.S. Civil War began, both France and Great Britain had ironclad warships in service and others in production. The naval battles of the Civil War are unique because advances in technology changed the effectiveness of naval ships and tactics during the course of the war. The most obvious example is the battle between the ironclads *Merrimack* and *Monitor*.

AMERICAN IRONCLADS

The South needed a powerful warship, and they acquired it in an unlikely way. When the state of Virginia seceded in 1861, federal military and naval bases in that state suddenly found themselves in enemy territory. The men at the naval base at what is now the Norfolk Naval Shipyard received orders to destroy and abandon the facility to keep the Confederacy from seizing the ships, arms, and supplies there. One of the ships at the base was the USS *Merrimack*, a steam-powered frigate. The Federals set the *Merrimack* on fire, but it sank before the blaze inflicted too much damage. The Confederates managed to salvage the engines and hull of the *Merrimack* and outfitted the ship with iron armor. After hearing of Northern plans to construct their own ironclad, the Confederate navy added a ram to the vessel to sink enemy ships. The Confederacy renamed the ship CSS *Virginia*, although it is still commonly referred to as the *Merrimack*.

Meanwhile, Union engineers set out to build a new kind of warship, one unlike any other. In August 1861, Navy officials approached John Ericsson, a Swedish immigrant whom the Navy had refused to pay for work done on the USS *Princeton* after the explosion of a cannon on the ship in 1844 killed the secretary of state and the secretary of the Navy. Although the explosion was not because of Ericsson's work on the ship, political maneuverings forced him to quit building ships for the U.S. Navy. Despite this tragedy in his past, Ericsson overcame his pride and began to work on his innovative warship, the USS *Monitor*.

Ericsson's ship sat low in the water, with only the armored deck visible. A round turret was positioned on the deck. According to historian Bruce Catton, some observers said that the *Monitor* "looked like a tin can on a shingle." The appearance of Ericsson's ship was unconventional, and the ship contained important new technologies. Steam power rotated the turret. The *Monitor* was, in fact, one of the first ships powered entirely by steam, thanks to Ericsson's invention, the marine screw. The ship's smokestack was detachable, and the entire craft was protected by armor plates.

Ericsson did his best to protect his ironclad. He placed most of the ship below water. Only the pilothouse and the turret remained above the waterline. These features made the *Monitor* the first semisubmersible ship. As Union workers raced to complete the *Monitor*, Confederate workers finished outfitting their own ironclad. Each side knew that the other was trying to develop an unbeatable warship, and each side wanted to be the first to launch its new weapon. According to historian Bern Anderson,

> Early in 1862 tension on both sides increased as both *Merrimack* and *Monitor* neared completion. So great was the pressure [by Southern war leaders] to get *Merrimack* into action before *Monitor* appeared that when the ship got under way for the first time on March 8, the crew thought that they were merely going on a trial run.

The crew soon learned, however, that this maiden voyage was anything but a trial run. Captain Franklin Buchanan led the new ship to the Chesapeake Bay, to Hampton Roads, Virginia. There, the *Merrimack* boldly attacked the Union fleet.

THE *MERRIMACK* AND THE *MONITOR*

Although it was not a new idea, the use of ironclads by both the Union and the Confederacy demonstrated that wooden naval ships were dead. Ships made of wood were no match for even small ironclads with small guns. The era of wooden warships was over.

The revolving turret was another important advancement introduced with the *Monitor*-class ironclads. A revolving turret was a round, can-shaped tower that rotated horizontally. With guns mounted inside its turret, the ship could fire in any direction. This eliminated the need to maneuver the ship into position before it could fire on an enemy target. This also meant that any guns on the ship could be brought into position by rotation and directed against the enemy, rather than just the guns on one side of the ship, as in frigates and ships of the line.

Thus, even though the USS *Monitor* had limited firepower, its turret allowed it to hold its own in an artillery duel with the *Merrimack*. The *Merrimack*, with guns on its sides, had to position itself to fire on an enemy ship. The *Monitor* merely needed to turn its turret and commence firing. This technological innovation was so effective that modern naval, air, and tank artillery guns all retain this feature. The *Monitor* had just two guns mounted within its revolving turret. In contrast, the *Merrimack* boasted 10 guns and two howitzers. Despite its superior firepower, the *Merrimack* was an example of the traditional warship, in which half of the guns were placed on each side. This design reflected naval technology before the war and older naval strategy that called for broadside artillery duels between ships.

The first battle ever to take place between two ironclads occurred during the Battle of Hampton Roads, March 8 and 9, 1862. Although the *Merrimack* was not quite ready for combat, the commander ordered the ship to accompany a small fleet of Confederate ships as they prepared to engage the Union fleet. The *Merrimack* immediately attacked the Union fleet by ramming a Union frigate, the USS *Cumberland*. The ironclad's ram struck the frigate below the waterline with such force that the *Cumberland* immediately began to sink. The *Merrimack* was unable to withdraw its ram before the weight of the sinking *Cumberland* tore the ram from the ironclad.

Next, the *Merrimack* attacked another Union frigate, the USS *Congress*. After witnessing the quick death of the *Cumberland*, the captain of the *Congress* ordered his ship to shallow water to prevent it from being rammed. Unfortunately, the maneuver prevented the *Congress* from escaping. The crew of the *Congress* could do little as several Confederate ships opened fire on the isolated ship. After an hour of withstanding a fierce bombardment, the *Congress* surrendered. The surviving Union crewmembers began to evacuate the ship. As boats ferried the survivors to shore, a Union gun fired on the *Merrimack*. The ironclad responded by firing an incendiary shell into the *Congress*, setting the ship on fire. When the flames reached the powder magazine, the resulting explosion destroyed the ship.

The *Merrimack* then turned its attention to the USS *Minnesota*, which tried to escape and then ran aground on a sandbar. Although the Union ship was virtually helpless, the shallow water prevented the *Merrimack* from destroying it. As the first day of the battle ended, the *Merrimack* had established its dominance over the Union fleet. The *Merrimack* had suffered damage, however. In addition to losing its ram, the ship had two inoperative guns. The ironclad also lost some of its steam-power because of damage to its smokestack. A number of the ship's protective armor plates were loose, as well. Despite the damage to their ship, the crew of the *Merrimack* had performed brilliantly. The ship itself had done exactly what the Confederacy wanted and needed. The *Merrimack* retired for the night and made plans to complete its mission the next day.

The dominance of the *Merrimack* lasted for a single day. During the night, the USS *Monitor* reached Hampton Roads and prepared to take on the South's ironclad. On the morning of March 9, 1862, the first clash between two ironclads took place. The *Monitor* was a smaller ship, but it could move more quickly through the water than its Confederate rival. Each ship landed shots on the other. Both ships withstood the shots, and neither ship suffered serious damage. The *Monitor* then withdrew for a short time; when it returned, the *Merrimack* retreated. The first battle between ironclads was a draw. Strategically, the North maintained its blockade of Southern ports. Significantly, the battle of the ironclads demonstrated that wooden ships no longer were capable of providing adequate defense. The age of ironclads and metal ships had arrived.

DESTRUCTION OF THE REBEL MONSTER "MERRIMAC" OFF CRANEY ISLAND MAY 11 1862

Ironclads like the Merrimack *and the* Monitor *were faster and more effective weapons in the water, and a showdown between the two titans marked the beginning of a new era in naval combat. The ships met at the Battle of Hampton Roads in a confrontation that ended in a draw. Afterwards, Confederate troops destroyed the* Merrimack *(above) to prevent the Union from seizing it.*

During the next two months, the *Merrimack* steamed to Hampton Roads, attempting to engage in another battle with the *Monitor*. Because the Union navy feared losing its greatest weapon (and its only deterrent to the *Merrimack*) the U.S. Navy ordered its ironclad to remain in port. Neither the *Merrimack* nor the *Monitor* ever entered combat again. When Union troops occupied Norfolk on May 10, 1862, the Confederates had no place to take their ironclad. Rather than allow the *Merrimack* to fall into Union hands, on May 11, the Confederates ran the ironclad aground and set it afire. When the fire reached the ship's magazine, an explosion destroyed the *Merrimack*.

Meanwhile, the *Monitor* served as the model for a new class of warship. The Union used the *Monitor*-class ships throughout the remainder of the war on rivers in both the Eastern and Western Theaters of Operations. The ships were effective on rivers, but the craft were not designed for the open sea. The heavy turret made a *Monitor*-class ship top heavy, and its low profile

The *Monitor's* Turret

The design of the USS *Monitor* included several new technological features. One of these was its rotating turret. Despite the advantages the turret provided to the ironclad, there were some faults in the original design. The interior diameter of the turret was just under 20 feet (6 meters). This space cramped the crew and the ship's two Dahlgren guns. The largest problem came with the portholes through which the guns fired. The *Monitor's* designer, John Ericsson, developed a system whereby iron shutters covered the ports when the guns were not firing or extended through the ports. This feature was intended to protect the crew from taking a direct hit into the turret while the guns were being reloaded. In practice, however, the crew found the metal shutters awkward and difficult to operate. Rather than struggle with the shutters, the men simply turned the turret away from enemy fire to reload.

When the *Monitor* sank in the Atlantic on the last day of 1862, the Union lost its first ironclad. Marine researchers discovered the ship in 1973. The U.S. government designated the shipwreck as its first National Marine Sanctuary. In August 2002, the National Oceanic and Atmospheric Administration (NOAA) retrieved the turret and took it to the Mariners' Museum in Newport News, Virginia, where the USS *Monitor* Center is located. Researchers placed the turret in a conservation tank, where it will remain for several more years. Visitors to the center can see other *Monitor* artifacts retrieved from the ocean floor and view a full-size replica of the *Monitor*.

in the water made it susceptible to being swamped by waves. In December 1862, the USS *Rhode Island* was towing the *Monitor* along the coast to help blockade the Carolinas. The ships ran into a storm off Cape Hatteras, North Carolina. The *Monitor*, which sat low in the water, took on water and then sank on December 31. The Union's first ironclad was lost in the Atlantic Ocean.

LATER IRONCLADS

The South did not have the industrial capabilities and technological skills to produce their own ironclads. Instead, the Confederate States of America tried to purchase ironclad warships from Great Britain. The Union blockade kept the South from ever receiving any of the ordered ironclads, however. The blockade held and contributed to the Union victory in 1865. After the success of the *Monitor*, the Union constructed many more ironclads patterned after their first one. The United States had 58 such ships in production or completed at the war's end.

The battle between the *Monitor* and the *Merrimack* convinced naval strategists around the world that wooden ships were obsolete for naval combat. Soon, the world's navies began to construct their own ironclads. This drive for naval supremacy led to the development of battleships, which were warships made completely of metal. The battle also led to the development of larger and more powerful naval guns.

Under the Sea

One of the areas in which technology advanced significantly during the Civil War was in naval warfare. In addition to adding armor to warships, both the North and the South looked for ways to gain a tactical advantage by developing new kinds of watercraft. The Union blockade, which stretched along more than 3,500 miles of coastline, forced the Confederacy to search for ways to break through. The South lacked the resources it needed to compete in traditional naval engagements with the North. Although Southern blockade-runners conducted trade in defiance of Northern forces, the blockade became more effective with each passing month of the war.

At first, many believed that the logistics of the task prevented the North from imposing an effective blockade on the Confederacy. Despite the vast size of the undertaking, however, the Union blockade eventually placed the South in a stranglehold that hurt the Confederate war effort. Confederate military leaders looked for an innovative weapon that might force the

North to release its grip on Southern ports. Lacking the natural resources necessary for waging a modern war, the South turned to an old idea that had not yet worked: the submarine.

A submarine is a watercraft that can travel underwater and operate independently. Before the Civil War, submarines were mostly just a concept. The necessities of war, however, caused the South to look for ways to break the Union blockade, and the submarine seemed to fit the bill. Throughout the nineteenth century, inventors and engineers constructed experimental submarines. Many of these experiments were focused on the military use of such craft. Submarine builders faced many obstacles, however. Getting a submarine to sink and then rise again in the water was a key difficulty. Through trial and error, submarine researchers found ways to make their craft sink and rise. To accomplish this, engineers added ballast tanks.

To understand how ballast tanks work, it is important to understand how metal ships (or submarines) float. To float, an object must weigh less than the amount of water that its volume displaces. A large metal submarine might weigh many pounds, but it will have buoyancy if the volume of water it displaces weighs more than the submarine itself. This is the basic concept that allows any metal ship to float.

A ballast tank is a compartment filled with air that can be used to add or subtract buoyancy to or from a boat or ship. For a submarine to sink, ballast, or weight, is added, usually by allowing water into the ballast tank. As the tank fills, the submarine becomes less buoyant and sinks. For the boat to rise, pumps must force the water back out of the tank. As the water is forced out the weight of the boat is lowered, and the craft's buoyancy increases. Early inventors of submarines had to devise ways to add and remove ballast to sink and raise their undersea boats.

EARLY SUBMARINES

Before the Civil War, there were several other attempts to use submarines for military purposes. The year 1776 marked the development of the first submarine for military use. David Bushnell designed and constructed a small, egg-shaped craft to hold just one man. Bushnell's submarine was used during the early stages of the American Revolutionary War, as the colonists suffered from an extended blockade of their major ports. The *Turtle*, as Bushnell called his submarine, relied on the man within it to provide the power to move the craft. He did this by means of a hand crank connected to screw propellers. Bushnell's creation became the first submarine craft to be launched and to function independently of another ship. An officer in the Continental army, Sergeant Ezra Long, operated the *Turtle*. On September 7, 1776, Long powered the small submarine within New York Harbor in a failed attempt to sink a British warship and end the blockade of the harbor. Bushnell later dismantled his invention.

In 1861, at the outbreak of the Civil War, the North devised the so-called Anaconda Plan to help it win the war. This plan depended on a strong Union navy to blockade Southern ports and win control of the Mississippi River. Because the South relied on outside supplies and materials, it lacked the ability to grow and provide for its own needs—especially the needs for waging war. If the North could prevent the South from using their seaports, the Union could squeeze the life out of the Confederacy. The plan was named for a large snake—the anaconda—that constricts itself around its prey to squeeze it to death.

Under the plan, just outside many Southern harbors, Union warships lay in wait. These naval vessels prevented the Confederacy from receiving materials from their trading partners. The blockade also kept the South from shipping cotton and other goods to overseas markets. The South could not send or receive the goods it needed to buy and sell to wage war against the North. There were strong opinions against the use of military submarines. Many people believed that submarines were an unfair way to wage war. Despite the prejudices against these

David Bushnell created the Turtle, the first functioning submarine in history, in an attempt to break the British naval blockade during the American Revolution. Made out of oak and iron bands, the underwater vessel was big enough for only one operator, who had to use a hand crank to move the submarine through the water. The Turtle also had a large screw meant to drill holes into the hulls of wooden ships for waterproof explosives. Above, the Turtle surfaces in New York Harbor in 1776.

new weapons of war, both the North and the South worked feverishly to produce a viable submarine for combat.

TORPEDOES

Today's torpedoes, called locomotive torpedoes, are self-propelled. Once launched, they can rush through the water on their own toward enemy ships. Torpedoes of the Civil War were not self-propelled. Instead, these early torpedoes were simply water mines. The forces of the North and South used various kinds of torpedoes. Some Civil War torpedoes were explosives attached to buoyant materials that floated at or below the surface of the water and were anchored to the bottom of a river channel or harbor. These devices were meant to discourage enemy ships from approaching. Electric cables connected each device to the shore. Defenders of the harbor or river port watched for enemy ships and triggered an explosion through the cable if a ship sailed too close to the torpedo. Although the threat of these torpedoes did prevent enemy ships from sailing upriver or within a harbor, the technology was not reliable. Often, the cable connection did not work, or the torpedo failed to explode or exploded too late to cause serious damage.

Another kind of torpedo floated on top of the water. These bombs contained an instrument that set off an explosion when it made contact with a hard object. Because there was no way to know what object might cause the torpedo to explode, these weapons were not effective. Defenders hoped that the torpedoes would damage or sink an enemy ship, but the weapons also posed a threat to the defenders' own ships. When the Confederates used these torpedoes, they sometimes hindered Union naval operations, but they did not break the blockade.

The third kind of torpedo involved submarines. Confederate operatives realized that they needed an accurate way to place a torpedo into direct contact with an enemy ship. To do this, Confederate engineers began to develop submarines. The engineers envisioned a silent, unseen, underwater craft equipped either with spar torpedoes (torpedoes that were attached to an enemy ship by means of a spar, or pole, that projected from the bow of the attacking craft) or torpedoes that were towed along behind the attacking craft. Such a submarine offered the prospect of breaking the blockade.

THE CSS *DAVID*

The Confederates developed an underwater boat for the specific purpose of delivering a torpedo to sink Union ships. The CSS *David* was a cigar-shaped wooden boat powered by steam. A Confederate citizen, T. Stoney, built the *David* at Charleston, South Carolina. After its completion, Stoney turned the boat over to the Confederate navy. The *David* was 50 feet long and held a crew of four. The new vessel sat low in the water, increasing the difficulty for enemy gunners to take aim at it. Defensively, part of its hull was fitted with iron sheeting. The boat was used only on dark nights. It burned anthracite coal, a coal that burns without smoke. The vessel delivered its torpedo by attaching its explosive payload to an enemy ship by means of a spar that projected from the *David*'s bow. The spar could carry a 60- to 70-pound explosive charge that was capable of inflicting serious damage on most Union ships. The *David* looked and operated much like a submarine. Despite these characteristics, however, the *David* was technically a surface vessel—a torpedo boat. Because its smokestack projected out of the water, the boat was too obvious to use during the day. Additionally, its steam engine made enough noise to limit its effectiveness at night. Still, the *David* was a ship that caused the Union to take extra precautions.

On October 5, 1863, just off Morris Island at Charleston Harbor, the *David,* commanded by Lieutenant William T. Glassell, quietly approached the Union ship USS *New Ironsides*, which lay at anchor. The *New Ironsides* was an impressive warship, one of the North's ironclad steamers. Glassell guided his boat to within 50 yards of the ironclad before a Union lookout detected the torpedo boat. The lookout called out to Glassell, who responded with a shotgun blast. Then, the Confederate ship delivered its payload: It detonated a spar torpedo under the Union ship.

The explosion caused a large wave and shower of water to engulf the *David*, extinguishing its boiler fires. The attacking

Confederate forces developed a torpedo boat (above), an underwater vessel that could attach explosives to Union ships. Powered by a small boiler, this ship was not as stealthy as a submarine due to its visible smokestack and rumbling engine. The Confederacy's first torpedo boat, the CSS David, conducted the first torpedo attack in 1863 against the USS New Ironsides.

ship did not sink, but it sat helpless in the water without its boiler fires. Union sailors peppered the vessel with small arms fire but caused no serious damage. Because Glassell was convinced that the *David* was sinking, he and two of his men abandoned the ship. One of the two returned to relight the boiler fires, however. The two remaining crewmembers returned safely to shore, but the Union captured Glassell and the other crewmember. Although the attack did some damage to the *New Ironsides*, the ironclad remained in use throughout the war. Glassell's shotgun blast inflicted the only fatal casualty of the attack.

Confederate forces built and operated several other *David*-class torpedo boats. Crews using the *Davids* managed to deliver torpedoes to Union ships. Despite some successes, however, the North's blockade continued to limit trade in and out of Southern ports. The Confederacy needed to find another way to torpedo Union warships. The South needed a ship that could avoid detection and still deliver a torpedo. The South needed something more than a torpedo boat. The South needed an invention not yet perfected—a submarine.

SOUTHERN SUBMARINE EFFORTS

The South found their submarine inventors in two unlikely men: Horace Lawson Hunley and James McClintock. Hunley was a plantation owner, a lawyer, and a customs official who was living in New Orleans, Louisiana, when the war broke out. Hunley's success as a businessman provided him with the financial resources to bankroll the Confederacy's submarine endeavor. James McClintock was trained as an engineer. He co-owned a New Orleans machine shop, where he made gauges for steam-powered equipment. His engineering and manufacturing experience helped prepare him to build a submarine.

The two men formed a partnership in an attempt to claim a prize. The Confederate States of America offered a $100,000 reward for the destruction of the USS *New Ironsides* or the USS *Wabash*. These two steam-powered Union ships boasted large guns and patrolled the Southern coast to enforce the blockade. The Confederate government also offered a $50,000 reward to anyone who managed to destroy a *Monitor*-class vessel. Hunley and McClintock hoped to claim such rewards with their submarine.

The Hunley Discovered

The Civil War ended the year after the *Hunley* sank outside Charleston Harbor. Many people searched unsuccessfully for the submarine in the years that followed. In May 1995, a team of researchers financed by novelist and underwater explorer Clive Cussler finally located the wreck. Cussler founded the National Underwater and Marine Agency (NUMA). The nonprofit organization is devoted to conserving maritime relics and artifacts by locating and preserving shipwrecks. The state of South Carolina established the *Hunley* Commission, which cooperated with a nonprofit organization called Friends of the *Hunley* to preserve the submarine and tell the story of the *Hunley* and its crew.

On August 8, 2000, 136 years after it sank, researchers raised the *Hunley*. The researchers have taken extraordinary measures to learn as much as they can about the submarine. They have placed the vessel in a freshwater tank to leech out the salt that accumulated during the boat's long stay underwater. (Salt damages iron.) They have sifted through harbor-bottom silt to retrieve any artifacts. They also have carefully removed human remains.

The researchers who raised the *Hunley* know that they have discovered an important historical artifact. They also know that they have discovered a war grave. Researchers have painstakingly removed each human bone from the silt and muck inside the submarine. After cleaning the bones, they have reassembled the skeletons. Forensic researchers have examined the remains to learn as much as possible about the crew. Other researchers have searched through genealogies and public records to determine the identity of each crewmember. After learning all that they could from the remains, the team made sure that the brave men of the *Hunley* received proper burial, 140 years after their deaths, on April 17, 2004. George Dixon and his crew of submariners were laid to rest with full military honors. Their remains lie in Charleston's Magnolia Cemetery.

At the outset of the war, McClintock and Hunley began to develop plans to construct a submarine. Hunley had the financial resources, and McClintock had the engineering knowledge. Hunley was a Southern patriot and a businessman. He wanted to see the South win the war and was determined to aid the war effort. The plantation owner also resented the Union blockade, which kept him from shipping his cotton and sugar crops to overseas markets. During the war, Hunley spent thousands of his own dollars in his quest to develop a military submarine capable of breaking the blockade.

In February 1863, after two failed attempts, Hunley and McClintock started work on their third submarine. To acknowledge Hunley's financial support for the project, McClintock named the submarine the *H.L. Hunley*. The *Hunley* was shaped like a fish; this prompted some observers to nickname it the "fish boat." The partners designed the *Hunley* to carry a torpedo and detonate it next to an enemy ship, in the manner of other torpedo boats. The crew propelled the craft using hand cranks. After construction was completed, Hunley and McClintock tested the boat's capabilities.

THE *H.L. HUNLEY*

General Dabney Maury observed the *Hunley* while its owners ran test runs in the harbor of Mobile Bay. Historian Sally M. Walker records that Maury, who commanded the Confederate forces in Mobile, Alabama, described the submarine as a ship that "towed a floated torpedo, dived under a ship, dragging the torpedo, which fairly exploded under the ship's bottom, and blew the fragments one hundred feet into the air." Maury and others immediately understood the tactical advantages that the *Hunley* offered. The vessel could approach Union ships without the tell-tale noise and smokestack of the *David*-class boats. The submarine also could place an explosive exactly when and where the crew desired. No longer would the South have to hope that an anchored torpedo might detonate against the hull of a Union ship. With the *Hunley*, the South could attack Northern ships at will. It appeared as if the Confederacy finally had the necessary weapon to break the Union blockade.

During a test run on August 29, either a careless mistake or a malfunction caused the submarine to dive unexpectedly while the boat's manholes were open. Water poured into the craft, causing it to descend rapidly. Five crewmembers drowned in the accident.

Responding to a lack of confidence in his craft, Hunley volunteered to command the submarine. On October 15, 1863, Hunley and his crew conducted tests during rainy and foggy weather. After one successful dive, the *Hunley* sank for the second time in less than seven weeks in Mobile Bay. This time, the sinking drowned the boat's namesake, H.L. Hunley, and his entire crew.

Many people, including General Beauregard, believed that a submarine was too dangerous to continue in development. The general ordered all submarine operations to cease. Two men, George E. Dixon and William Alexander, believed that the submarine could still work. The two determined that pilot error had caused the accident. Beauregard granted Dixon command of the *Hunley* in mid-November 1863, and ordered that the *Hunley's* combat missions were to be conducted on the surface.

Banned from diving during an attack, Dixon had to find another way to use the *Hunley* to deliver a torpedo. Dixon decided to install a torpedo spar, much like those that were fitted on the *David* boats. Dixon also had to recruit a new crew. William Alexander agreed to help and joined the crew. Knowing the risks, the rest of the crew volunteered from a Confederate ship. Including Dixon, eight men made up the final *Hunley* crew.

The *Hunley* slipped out of the harbor four nights a week. Traveling beneath the surface, the crew practiced approaching Union vessels in the dark and surfacing near the enemy ships. The crew continued to train through January. Dixon and his crew gained confidence in their mission. Dixon was ready to try out the submarine in combat.

On February 17, 1864, a Union sailor spied the strange-looking object in the water as it approached his ship. He alerted an officer, who dismissed the object as a floating log. Another officer also saw the *Hunley* and called out an alarm. Meanwhile, onboard the submarine, Dixon's crew increased the speed of their craft by cranking faster. Union sailors fired at the submarine, but their firearms did no serious damage. With a torpedo spar protruding from its bow, the submarine hurtled toward the warship. The *Hunley*'s spar struck the hull of the *Housatonic*, creating a hole in the ship's hull. The *Hunley* had successfully delivered the torpedo.

After depositing the torpedo, Dixon and his crew reversed their cranking and pulled away from the *Housatonic*. When they had reached the proper distance, Dixon pulled the line that detonated the torpedo. An explosion rocked the Union ship. The *Housatonic* tilted to one side and quickly began to sink. Within five minutes, the ship touched bottom. The warship had been sunk in 28 feet of water. Tall masts reaching out of the water marked the *Housatonic*'s resting place.

Confederate observers on the shore believed that the *Hunley* signaled them. They lit a signal fire, and waited jubilantly for the victorious submarine to return to shore. The *Hunley* never returned from its successful mission, however. The fate of the submarine remained a mystery for more than 130 years, until researchers discovered the wreck of the vessel in the muck of the seafloor outside Charleston Harbor in 1995.

Although Dixon and his crew never returned to shore, the *Hunley* holds the distinction of being the first submarine to sink an enemy ship in combat. The deed foreshadowed technological advances that forever changed the course of naval warfare. Civil War submarines failed to live up to expectations, but the lessons learned led to the development of submarines for military, scientific, and salvaging uses in the coming decades.

UNION SUBMARINES

The Union viewed such submarines as useful tools for clearing underwater obstacles in Southern ports and rivers. The first submarine commissioned into service in the U.S. Navy was a boat invented by Brutus de Villeroi, an immigrant from France.

De Villeroi's submarine had two features that were new to submarines and that are important enough to be used today. The first was an air-purifying system that removed the carbon dioxide from the air. This extended the time the craft could remain submerged. No other submarine from that era had such a modern feature. The second feature allowed a diver to exit the craft through an air lock while it was submerged.

In the spring of 1862, the Navy dispatched its new submarine to Hampton Roads, Virginia. There, the Navy intended to use the submarine and its crew of 14 civilians and one commissioned officer to destroy a railroad bridge that spanned Appomattox River. The railway served as a major supply line to Richmond, the capital of the Confederacy. A local newspaper reporter observed the green craft moving slowly through the water, propelled by oars. He described it as looking like an alligator. The description was appropriate, and others began to call the submarine the "alligator." The nickname stuck, and the Navy christened the vessel *Alligator*.

The first and only combat assignment for the *Alligator* did not go well. The Navy wanted the submarine to approach the railroad-bridge supports underwater. At the bridge, a diver was to exit the craft through an air lock and place mines on the span's supporting beams. After the diver returned to the submarine, the crew would use a battery to detonate the explosives. The crew of the *Alligator* never got the chance to attempt their mission, however. Union officials feared that the submarine would be visible to the Confederates in the shallow waters.

In late March 1863, the USS *Sumpter* towed the *Alligator* southward in the Atlantic toward South Carolina. On April 2,

Determined to break the Union's naval blockade, Louisiana businessman H. L. Hunley funded the efforts of engineers James McClintock and Baxter Watson. Together, these men built three submarines for the Confederacy: the Pioneer, *the* American Diver, *and the* H. L. Hunley. *Despite two fatal accidents aboard the* H. L. Hunley (above), *the ship was the first submarine to successfully attack and sink another vessel, the Union's* Housatonic.

1863, the *Sumpter* encountered a violent Atlantic storm. The fury of the storm damaged the submarine, and it began to fill with water. Admiral DuPont, in command of the *Sumpter*, feared that the submarine would sink and take his ship down with it. DuPont ordered the towlines cut, and the *Alligator* slipped beneath the waves. Although researchers have made efforts to locate the craft, it has not yet been found.

Although Northern naval capabilities were focused primarily on ironclads, the Federals did work to produce one other submarine during the war. The *Intelligent Whale* was just under

29 feet long and carried a crew of 6 to 13 men. The craft was propelled by hand. Horizontal and vertical rudders allowed the crew to maneuver the submarine. The *Intelligent Whale* also featured doors located on the bottom. These allowed a diver to exit the craft to plant explosives. Engineers did not successfully complete the *Intelligent Whale* project before the end of the war, however. After the war, the U.S. Navy conducted tests on the *Intelligent Whale*. These revealed that the craft was anything but leakproof. The U.S. Navy abandoned their efforts, and the *Intelligent Whale* never saw action.

The use of submarines in the Civil War did not alter the outcome of that conflict. Nevertheless, the ideas suggested and the advances made during the war led to future innovations that forever changed the nature of naval warfare. The potential for submarines to tip the balance of power was evident, and nations around the globe began to research and develop their own submarines. In conflicts that followed the Civil War, warring countries used submarines as part of their naval arsenal.

Medicine

O ne key statistic of the Civil War was the increase in the number of battlefield fatalities. Advances in technology outpaced advances in military tactics, resulting in many unnecessary injuries and deaths. Worse still, medical professionals did not yet know about germs. At the time of the Civil War, concepts and standards of sanitation and sterilization were quite different from modern standards. According to Civil War historian James M. McPherson, "Disease was the principal killer of Civil War soldiers." Both armies struggled to care for their wounded. Author Peter J. Parish claims, however, that "the medical services represent one of the Civil War's most dismal failures." Indeed, government bureaucracy, inept surgeons, and lack of knowledge certainly contributed to poor conditions. As James M. McPherson notes, however, *"By the standards of the time*, Civil War medical care and army health were unusually good."

Both sides in the Civil War made use of many technologies that affected medical care for soldiers. Railroads consistently carried food and other supplies to armies. Because of this reliable means of supply, the large armies on both sides were able to remain on the front year round. Advances in weaponry increased the capability of soldiers to inflict and receive battlefield injuries. Railroads enabled armies to evacuate wounded soldiers in numbers far greater than in previous wars. This meant that wounded men who might have died on the battlefield in earlier wars soon found themselves in hospitals away from the front. Suddenly, large numbers of wounded soldiers needed care. Both sides, but especially the North, took steps to treat their wounded. Thus, although no medical breakthroughs occurred during the war, the conflict did spur an important improvement in the medical care of soldiers. Military medical services expanded greatly during the war. By 1863, the U.S. Army Medical Corps was professionalized.

BATTLEFIELD MEDICAL CARE

One of the most amazing innovations to take place during the war was the way in which the Union attempted to treat its wounded. Union officials created a medical transport system that other countries copied and duplicated in the years following the Civil War. This system evacuated men away from the battlefield and delivered them to nearby field hospitals to provide medical care.

At the beginning of the war, the evacuation of wounded soldiers was a confusing mess. This resulted in many men failing to receive necessary medical care. An army doctor named Jonathan Letterman soon revolutionized battlefield care. Dr. Letterman was a surgeon serving with the Army of the Potomac. In June 1862, Letterman received appointment as the medical director of the Army of the Potomac, holding the rank of major. General George McClellan, who commanded the Army of the Potomac, authorized Letterman to make any necessary changes to improve battlefield medical care.

The 38-year-old doctor quickly reorganized the medical services for the force. The changes took time to put into practice. Little progress was evident during the Seven Days Battles, which were fought just after Letterman received his appointment. In September, however, at the Battle of Antietam, Dr. Letterman's genius was plain. The doctor employed a system of first-aid stations near the front, assigned to each regiment. At the stations, medical personnel ranked the severity of each wounded soldier and determined the level of care needed. Stretcher bearers helped carry wounded to these stations when possible. Farther behind the lines, near the division and corps headquarters, Letterman set up his field hospitals. Medical supplies were distributed from the field hospitals to the areas on the battlefield where they were needed. An ambulance corps operated between the first-aid stations and the field hospitals.

The ambulance corps fulfilled the simple yet important function of relocating the wounded from the battlefield to the field hospitals. To make the system more efficient, commanders assigned specific soldiers to ambulance duty. The men assigned to ambulance duty used stretchers and wagons to carry the wounded to help. Medical doctor and author Alfred Jay Bollet describes how stretchers, or litters, were "improvised from available materials, including poles through the sleeves of coats, gates removed from fences, window shutters, doors, ladders, blankets lashed to poles," and virtually anything else soldiers could find to get their wounded comrades to the medical personnel. Modern ambulances are large vehicles with all the necessary equipment to administer aid. In contrast, Civil War ambulances were simply vehicles that carried the wounded away from the battlefield. The introduction and organization of an ambulance corps allowed most soldiers to remain in the fight while others provided aid to their wounded fellow warriors, thereby maintaining troop strength.

Because so many men received battle wounds in the war, medical workers developed a system to rank the seriousness of

As medical director for the Army of the Potomac, Dr. Jonathan Letterman designed an efficient system that allowed wounded soldiers to be assessed and treated in order to return them to the battlefield as quickly as possible. Above, General George McClellan *(sixth from left),* Letterman *(eighth from left)* and the Army of the Potomac meet President Lincoln *(center).*

the injury. Today, such a system is called *triage*, from a French word that means "sorting." Generally, the medics made decisions to save those men who were most likely to recover. If a medic believed that a soldier would not recover from his wounds, efforts were made to make that soldier as comfortable as possible. The ambulance corps either left such soldiers to die where they lay or evacuated them after all the other wounded. Men who suffered from less life-threatening injuries received initial treatment at field dressing stations. Usually, the field dressing stations were located just behind the lines, in a somewhat sheltered area. These stations were often within range of enemy artillery, however. Workers then transported these wounded by ambulance to a field hospital, which usually was located well behind the lines. Finally, if possible, medical units removed those wounded men who suffered the most severe and likely fatal wounds.

The triage system appears somewhat subjective, especially for men who receive the worst injuries. Such a system gives those with lesser injuries a better chance of survival, however. Medical personnel use similar methods today when treating people wounded in war or injured in natural disasters.

In December 1862, at the Battle of Fredericksburg, the Union army had nearly 10,000 wounded soldiers. Letterman and his ambulance corps effectively cared for the wounded. After Fredericksburg, Letterman's system was put into operation in the other Union armies. At Gettysburg, in early July 1863, Letterman and his corps cared for nearly 21,000 wounded men (14,000 Federals and 6,800 Confederates). To handle the large number of injured, the corps set up an immense field hospital and camp, known as Camp Letterman. In March 1864, Congress mandated the triage system as the battlefield medical course of action for the U.S. Army. Today, Letterman is known as the Father of Battlefield Medicine. He is buried in Arlington National Cemetery.

ANESTHESIA

Anesthesia was one of the areas in which soldiers received state-of-the art medical care during the Civil War. Anesthesia is a total or partial loss of feeling that is generated by a drug. Throughout history, medical doctors have experimented with various kinds of anesthetics. Two of the early chemical anesthetics were chloroform and ether. In 1846, ether was introduced as an anesthetic for use during surgery. The drug rendered a patient unconscious and removed the pain during surgery. Some doctors resisted the use of anesthesia because they believed that pain was an aid in healing. The Civil War was not the first war in which surgeons used anesthetics. It was, however, the first war in which anesthetics found widespread use in treating the wounded. During the war, there were few operations in which the patient did not receive some form of anesthesia. Union and Confederate doctors both used chloroform and ether as anesthetics, although the South often suffered from a shortage of such painkillers.

PLASTIC SURGERY

Perhaps the most remarkable medical advance was the introduction of reconstructive, or plastic, surgery. Some doctors attempted such surgeries to aid soldiers who faced social exclusion because of disfiguring wounds. American society often mistreated people with injuries and disabilities. As writer Alfred Jay Bollet points out, "Although gratitude toward Civil War veterans lessened the stigma, disfigured soldiers knew they faced discrimination at home and in the workplace." Some wounded soldiers returned home to broken engagements after suffering amputations and other severe injuries.

Wishing to help soldiers who already faced long odds, some surgeons on both sides began to perform reconstructive surgeries. These operations were called plastic surgeries then as they are now. Some of the more complex cases required multiple operations, performed over several months. Civilian doctors adopted the techniques and methods used by military surgeons in plastic surgeries during the war. All such surgeries performed by Union doctors were attempts to reconstruct portions of the face: eyelids, noses, cheeks, lips, and chins. Some medical procedures required the aid of dentists, who provided false palates and teeth for injured patients. Medical doctor and author Alfred Jay Bollet recorded an instance in which a surgeon used skin flaps from the forehead of a disfigured veteran to reconstruct the veteran's nose and cheek. The patient first reported that when he touched his reconstructed nose, he felt the touch on his forehead. After just a few weeks, however, the patient reported that he felt the touch on the nose. Although plastic surgery could not restore appearances fully, the procedures did help to make the injuries less noticeable.

DRUGS AND MEDICINES

During the Civil War, medical knowledge was limited. In many ways, medical care during the conflict resembled medical care from the Middle Ages, hundreds of years before, more than it resembled medical care today. Doctors did the best they could with the tools they had and the knowledge they had inherited. The resulting medical care offered mixed results. On one hand, medical care improved as the war continued. On the other hand, that same care sometimes did more harm than good. Although some of the drugs and medicines of the period helped patients, others hurt patients. These drugs and medicines included morphine, opium, quinine, and mercury. To understand the use of certain drugs, it is important to describe the symptoms that doctors attempted to treat.

One of the chronic ailments of soldiers on both sides was diarrhea. Untreated, the condition can worsen and lead to dysentery, a disease that can result in severe dehydration and death. To treat diarrhea and pain, Civil War doctors used narcotics such as opium and morphine. Opium treated diarrhea effectively, but it also proved to be highly addictive. During the war, opium was available in pills, as powder, and mixed with alcohol.

Another narcotic, morphine, was given to lessen pain. Morphine came in pill or powder form and could be administered by injection or dissolved in a solution. Battlefield

The use of new weapons in the Civil War resulted in horrible cases of amputations and disfiguring injuries. In the field, military doctors did their best to treat the injured, but the number of wounded soldiers soon overwhelmed medical personnel. Because troops with disabilities often were stigmatized after the war, some surgeons began to perform reconstructive surgery to help them. Above, a medical team performs a battlefield amputation in a tent hospital.

conditions often led to limited supplies. Doctors usually had no syringes with which to inject medicines. To treat a patient, a doctor often used his fingers to apply morphine powder directly onto a wound. Opium and morphine were strong drugs

that proved to relieve pain, and both armies used them gener-
ously to treat their wounded.

To fight fevers, especially fevers that signified disease,
army doctors turned to quinine. Quinine comes from the bark
of the cinchona tree, which is found in South America. Europeans had used quinine in its raw form since the seventeenth century. French researchers first discovered how to extract quinine
from the raw material in 1817. During the Civil War, the Union
army used quinine as a preventative measure against malaria
and as a treatment of the disease if it was contracted. During
the Vicksburg campaign, malaria was a constant threat because
of the warm climate and swampy geography of the area. Surgeon General William A. Hammond directed all soldiers in
General Grant's army to take a daily dose of quinine. Many
soldiers resisted taking the medicine each day. To counter this
resistance, doctors mixed the quinine with whiskey, popular-
izing the daily dose.

Southern doctors also understood the value of quinine and
used it as a preventative measure with their troops. The Union
blockade caused a shortage of the drug, however, and led the
Confederates to search for other treatments. The shortage hurt
not only Southern troops in the field, but also civilians at home
because quinine was the common treatment for malaria even
before the war. Civilians and Southern doctors experimented
with various plants and herbs but found none to be as effective
as quinine. For much of the war, shortages forced most of the
South to get by with little quinine.

The use of mercury in medicines was common before
the Civil War. Mercury eventually was proved to be harmful,
but many doctors at the time did not know it. Surgeon General Hammond became convinced that mercury was too toxic
for human use. He prohibited the use of compounds containing mercury. This ban led to a backlash. Opponents within
the army medical community looked for ways to discredit
Hammond by drumming up vague charges against him. As

a result, Hammond faced a court-martial. He was convicted and removed from his post. The former surgeon general retired to New York, where he studied neurology and taught college and university classes. In 1879, Hammond appealed his court-martial. The conviction was overturned, in part, because by that time, medical science had validated his earlier conclusion: Compounds containing mercury posed harm to patients.

The Medicine of Death

Although advances in medicine helped surgeons save lives on the battlefield, some soldiers still died. Doctors and nurses did all they could for wounded soldiers. Other doctors drew from increased medical knowledge to preserve bodies after death. The practice of embalming increased rapidly during the war.

Before 1861, improvements in embalming techniques allowed some doctors to preserve bodies using chemicals. The high cost of embalming prevented all but the wealthy from considering such a procedure, however. Like so many other aspects of American life, the Civil War changed attitudes toward embalming and the affordability of the practice. At least three factors contributed to the increased demand for embalming during the war. First, the war produced a high number of deaths. Second, the battlefields were located at great distances from the homes of fighting men. Grieving families wanted to be able to bury their dead in family plots. Embalming made such burials, and even funeral services, possible. Third, a well-publicized embalming early in the war popularized the procedure.

Dr. Thomas Holmes is known as the Father of American Embalming. He gained fame after embalming Colonel Elmer E.

NURSING

Out of necessity, the nursing profession developed rapidly during the Civil War. The number of wounded soldiers placed heavy demands on medical personnel, who had to care for injuries, disease, and illness. Both civilian and military medical care in 1860 were appalling. Hospitals were unsanitary, nurses usually were concerned family members or friends rather than professionals, and most medical personnel knew nothing about

Ellsworth, a friend of President Abraham Lincoln. Ellsworth was shot and killed while attempting to remove a Confederate flag from a building in Alexandria, Virginia, on May 24, 1861. Holmes offered to embalm Ellsworth's body free of charge. President Lincoln agreed, and Dr. Holmes carried out the procedure at the Washington Navy Yard. The public viewing impressed many of Washington's elite, including the president's wife, Mary Todd Lincoln. As historian James C. Lee wrote, "When Mrs. Lincoln viewed the body, she found Ellsworth's face as natural as if he were merely enjoying a brief and pleasant sleep." Word of the embalming spread. Soon, families across the North were seeking similar services for their loved ones.

At first, the cost to embalm a man killed in battle was $25 for an enlisted man and $50 for an officer. The prices increased to $30 and $80, respectively, later in the war. Many embalmers also sold coffins to increase their profits. Because Union families often wanted to bury their loved ones close to home, it was not uncommon for railroads to carry remains northward from Southern battlefields. Holmes later claimed to have embalmed over 4,000 bodies during the war, although the number seems somewhat exaggerated.

The practice of embalming increased after the war. When John Wilkes Booth shot and killed Abraham Lincoln in April 1865, Mrs. Lincoln insisted that her husband's body be embalmed, a first for a president. A train carried Lincoln's preserved remains across the North before the president was interred in Springfield, Illinois.

proper sanitation and hygiene. During the Crimean War, which was fought between 1854 and 1856, British nursing pioneer Florence Nightingale demonstrated the need for competent nursing care for wounded soldiers. When war broke out in 1861 in the United States, a Massachusetts reformer named Dorothea Dix decided that it was time for a change in American medical practices. Her efforts revolutionized American nursing.

Dorothea Dix helped form a medical relief association that later became the U.S. Sanitary Commission. Dix asked the War Department for permission to supply 100 nurses to army hospitals in Washington, D.C., to provide proper care and cleanliness. The War Department ignored her. Dix did not give up, however. She petitioned members of the president's cabinet, insisting that the government take steps to reform medical care. Her persistence paid off, and the U.S. government authorized her to form a women's nursing corps.

Dix soon had 100 nurses caring for the wounded. The nurses' training included learning how to create makeshift crutches and splints and how to make bandages from cornhusks. The training was effective. Dix's nurses helped establish the need for professional nurses in medical care for both soldiers and civilians. The women performed so well that the prevailing attitude against women as supervisors in the medical field began to change. In addition to Dix's association, other organizations and orders of religious sisters provided women to care for the wounded. Dix, however, was perceived as abrasive, and the army eventually took more control of her nursing staff.

HOSPITAL SHIPS

Another use of technology in medical care during the Civil War came from an unlikely source: a ship. The Union captured a Confederate steamer in 1862, renamed it USS *Red Rover*, and converted it into a naval hospital ship. Renovations to the ship

Changing attitudes during the Civil War created a pharmaceutical industry in the United States, signaling a growing acceptance of pain-killers and anesthesia. Although little was known about these medications, quinine, opium, and morphine were administered to soldiers to counteract the effects of fevers, malaria, and pain. After the war, many of these drugs became popular with the public, encouraging further research and development of new medicines. Above, an advertisement for quinine.

included features designed to ensure comfort and provide sanitary conditions for its patients. The renovations included a fully equipped operating room, a steam boiler for doing laundry, an elevator, separate kitchens and dining areas for patients and medical staff, several bathrooms, and improved air circulation. Stationed on the Mississippi River, the 650-ton *Red Rover* boasted a medical staff of military doctors and volunteer female nurses from the Sisters of the Holy Cross, a Catholic order. These nurses were the first women to serve aboard a U.S. Navy ship.

Initially, the Union army directed the *Red Rover*. Later, the Navy assumed command of the vessel. The ship transported sick and wounded soldiers to cities and hospitals to receive better care. The *Red Rover* also carried medical supplies to other Union ships stationed on rivers in the Western Theater of Operations. The ship was, of course, a floating hospital that was capable of providing quality care to the wounded and sick. To treat patients with contagious diseases such as smallpox, the Navy anchored barges along the river. In this way, the *Red Rover* could supply the barges with the necessary supplies and isolate the contagious patients to prevent the spread of disease.

During the course of its military service, the *Red Rover* housed more than 2,400 patients. When the war ended, the U.S. government no longer had need of its first hospital ship. The Navy decommissioned the *Red Rover* on November 17, 1865. Twelve days later, the government sold the ship at public auction.

MEDICS AS NONCOMBATANTS

Technology helped armies inflict greater numbers of injuries in battle, and this increased the need for medical staff. Commanders altered long-held practices to adjust to the changing realities of war. As the Civil War progressed, people on both sides changed their views of doctors. Initially, captured doctors became prisoners of war. They received treatment similar to that given to any other captured soldiers. The situation changed in 1862, however, during Confederate general Thomas J. "Stonewall" Jackson's Valley Campaign.

During that campaign, the Union army set up a hospital in a Winchester, Virginia, hotel. When Confederate forces occupied the city, several Union doctors remained behind to continue caring for the wounded. General Jackson's surgeon, Dr. Hunter Holmes McGuire, proposed setting the doctors free, with no conditions. McGuire also suggested that the doctors might encourage the North to adopt a similar policy toward Southern medical personnel. General Jackson agreed, and the freed Union doctors returned to the North.

The next month, in the midst of the Peninsular Campaign, Union general George B. McClellan put forward a recommendation to his Southern counterpart, General Robert E. Lee, concerning captured doctors. McClellan asked that both sides treat all medical officers as noncombatants, and Lee agreed. McClellan then issued General Order No. 60, which stated, "The principle being recognized that medical officers shall not be held as prisoners of war, it is directed that all medical officers so held by the United States shall be immediately and unconditionally discharged." The next year, in Geneva, Switzerland, at the first international conference addressing the treatment of war prisoners, representatives from many countries adopted similar principles that viewed medical personnel as noncombatants.

This new point of view benefited both the Union and the Confederacy. Surgeons no longer had to evade enemy soldiers or attempt to move injured soldiers. Instead, doctors could remain with the wounded, giving care without fear of capture. Physicians from a retreating army could stay behind with their wounded until after the advancing enemy force had cared for their own soldiers and could turn their attention to the enemy-wounded. Because the doctors of the advancing force did not have to care for enemy-wounded immediately, the quality of care increased for advancing and retreating armies alike. Generally, the agreement helped wounded soldiers on both sides. All of these advances led historian James M. McPherson to conclude that "the Civil War gave an important impulse to the modernization and professionalization of medicine."

Photography,
Balloons,
and Espionage

T he various technologies used by the North and the South relied on advances made in the years before the Civil War. In some cases, the technologies were the results of humankind's searches from earliest times. The desire to capture an everlasting image is evident in the art of every known ancient culture. The human wish to fly is seen in Greek mythology. These and other technologies became fashionable in the years immediately before the Civil War. In those years, photography and ballooning were in their infancy. The war served as a proving ground for the two technologies. Battlefield photography led to battlefield reporting, a staple in the modern world. Officials used balloons to conduct aerial reconnaissance, a task carried out today by satellites and unmanned flying drones.

Additionally, and as discussed previously, the use of some technologies created the need for still further advances. Because military leaders and civilians in both the Union and the Confederacy spoke English and used the telegraph, encryption—converting messages into code—became necessary to protect vital information. As a result, the art of espionage—spying—reached new levels of sophistication. Government and military officials invented new methods and devices to keep their secrets, and spies devised new ways to find out those secrets and communicate them to their governments. The resourcefulness of agents and military commanders led to new uses of existing technologies and to the development of new technologies.

PHOTOGRAPHY

Photography rests on discoveries and inventions that date back 1,000 years. In the sixteenth century, scientists understood the concept of photography. People did not know which chemicals or other materials to use to produce a photograph, however. During the 1820s, Joseph Nicéphore Niépce, a French inventor, discovered how to make a permanent photographic image. Niépce worked with Louis Daguerre to find a chemical compound to shorten the exposure time needed to produce a photographic image. Niépce died in 1833, but Daguerre carried on the work.

In 1837, Daguerre successfully developed a system by which he captured an image on a mirror-polished surface. Named after its inventor, this permanent image was called the *daguerreotype*. In 1839, the French government purchased the patent from Daguerre and revealed the technology as a gift to the world. The technological process was quickly adopted across Europe and in the United States. Other inventors built on Daguerre's work. They added innovations that further decreased the necessary exposure time.

Another important advance was the introduction of glass negatives. These allowed people to make copies of photographs. In 1851, 10 years before the outbreak of the Civil War, an Englishman, Frederick Scott Archer, discovered the process for producing copies from glass negatives. Archer shared his findings with the world.

Although photography was still fairly new during the Civil War, both the North and the South made use of the technology in their efforts to win the war. In the Civil War, photography was used in mapmaking, in scouting the terrain, and in spying on the enemy. Spies armed with cameras found easy access to military encampments. The technology of photography was new enough that quite a few military men wanted to have their pictures taken. Many commanders did not realize the value of the information recorded in a photograph. According to author Donald E. Markle, at least one Union spy, Lafayette Baker, "took a broken camera with him on his trip south." Baker pulled off his trick. He raised suspicions only later, when no one received a photograph.

American photographer Mathew Brady was recognized internationally for his photographic work before the war. One of Brady's employees, photographer Alexander Gardner, worked as a Union spy for the famous detective and spy Allan Pinkerton. Gardner also photographed the countryside for Union generals. In exchange, he was given access to battlefields after the fighting ended.

Alexander Gardner also took group photographs of Union military units. Members of the units seemed to enjoy the prospect of having their photographs taken. More importantly, the unit commanders examined the finished photographs to identify possible Confederate spies. According to author Donald E. Markle, "The technique was so successful that Confederates attempting to infiltrate a unit were advised to never appear in any photographs."

Photography also had an impact on the home front. In October 1862, Mathew Brady opened an exhibit in his New York gallery. The name of the exhibit was "The Dead of Antietam." For the first time in history, American citizens saw photographs of dead American soldiers. Paintings of battlefield scenes usually showed soldiers dying nobly. In contrast, these authentic photographs showed corpses lying on the ground where they had fallen. Brady's exhibit made the war seem more real—and more horrific—to many Americans. The technology of photography helped to change the way people viewed the war. No longer was war a romantic undertaking. Instead, war was something to be dreaded, a necessary duty undertaken to preserve the Union.

Near the end of the war, Southern spies made use of an advanced form of photography that is an ancestor of today's microfilm. The spies condensed the written information they discovered and photographed it onto tiny glass negatives that measured just two square millimeters. To avoid detection, operatives carried the negatives southward inside hollow metal buttons on their clothing. Confederate officials used a strong lens to magnify and read the information.

Mathew Brady: Civil War Photographer

The most famous American photographer of the nineteenth century was Mathew Brady. When Brady was 29, his work won international acclaim at the first world's fair, which was held at London's Crystal Palace in 1851. Before the Civil War, in the 1840s and 1850s, Brady made a name for himself by photographing virtually every prominent American.

When the war began, Brady decided to photograph as much of it as he could. The photographer employed over twenty men to document the war on glass plates. Brady himself risked danger. He withstood enemy fire and barely escaped capture at the First Battle of Bull Run. His determination and actions made him one of the first photographers to chronicle America's history.

Photographers captured images of virtually every aspect of the war. These included images of battlefields, hospitals, encampments, the men of military units, their officers, and escaped and freed slaves. In many respects, these photographs recorded the day-to-day monotony of life at war. Taken together, the photographs make up an impressive and compelling record of the war. The technology of the day had a major limitation, however. Civil War–era photography lacked the ability to depict actual battles. Because of the required exposure times, the subjects of photographs in the 1860s needed to remain motionless from the time the camera's shutter was opened until it was shut. Some Civil War photographs appear to have ghostlike figures in them. These ghosts are the result of a person or animal moving while the shutter was open. Still, Mathew Brady and other Civil War photographers

Brady understood that his photographic missions involved financial risks as well, but he felt compelled to record the war in the only way he could. Brady believed that the government would want a photographic record of the war. He created more than 10,000 plates and spent over $100,000 photographing the war. When the war ended, the U.S. government and the American public wanted nothing more to do with the war, however.

Brady went bankrupt, and he lost his New York studio. Congress granted him $25,000 in 1875, but it was not enough to pull him out of debt. Mathew Brady died penniless in a charity ward in New York City in 1896. Despite his financial failure and the loss of his studio, Brady's work influenced later photographers. His images of war showed that the medium of photography could be used for more than simple, posed portraits. Photography could capture the human spirit and draw out emotions. Later photographers documented other wars using modern photographic technology. Even today photojournalists who cover wars follow in the steps of Mathew Brady.

Photography, a relatively new medium, was used for the first time in battle during the Civil War. The work of war photographers like Alexander Gardner (standing) proved to be useful in reconnaissance and espionage, as the recorded images allowed military officials to secretly preview battlefields, examine enemy camps, and detect enemy spies. Gardner also was able to capture the brutal nature of war in his photographs of Antietam.

produced an extraordinary record of war as it was never seen before. That record was made possible by the technology of photography.

BALLOONS

Balloonists, who were called aeronauts in the mid-nineteenth century, were nothing new in 1861. In 1783, French inventors developed balloons large enough to lift humans in baskets. The first large balloon relied on hot air to make it rise. Soon, however, someone discovered that hydrogen gas was sufficiently lighter than air to carry a large balloon into the sky. Indeed, hydrogen-filled balloons did not need to be as large as hot-air balloons to carry the same payload. Hot-air balloons held three distinct advantages over hydrogen, however. First, hot air was easier to produce than hydrogen. Nineteenth-century balloonists needed to combine thousands of pounds of iron filings with sulfuric acid to produce the amount of hydrogen needed to fill a balloon. Second, hot air is easier to use to make a balloon go up or down. A hot-air balloon operator could make the balloon rise or fall more quickly than a hydrogen-balloon operator. Third, hydrogen gas is extremely combustible: It easily explodes into flame. To fill a large balloon with a flammable gas was a dangerous undertaking. In contrast, a simple flame can produce hot air, and that flame poses no danger of sudden explosion. Despite the advantages of hot air over hydrogen, however, many early balloonists chose the explosive gas over hot air. The balloonists made this choice primarily because hydrogen can lift nearly 4.5 times the weight of an equal volume of hot air.

Civil War balloonists, and especially Confederate aeronauts, filled their balloons with coal gas instead of hydrogen. Coal gas was produced by the dry distillation of coal, which was used to light cities. Methane gas made up a large portion of coal gas. Although not as powerful as hydrogen, coal gas had more lifting power than hot air. Confederate balloonists relied on coal gas to lift their craft skyward.

Military planners saw the potential for balloons as tools with which to gather intelligence about the enemy. The French used balloons effectively during the French Revolution and when they fought against Austria in the 1790s. Balloonists observed troop movements, estimated troop strength, and reported to commanders on the ground about battlefield happenings as they occurred. The balloonists did this by means of notes attached to weights, which they dropped from the balloons. Between 1800 and the Civil War, several other countries used balloons to observe enemy troop movements. Other uses of balloons foreshadowed future uses of other sorts of air power. Some armies used balloons to distribute propaganda leaflets from the sky into besieged cities below. Some military balloonists successfully dropped small explosives. Many military planners resisted using the new technology, however. They preferred to rely on standard methods.

Beginning in the 1830s, civilian balloonists experimented with a variety of designs and propulsion methods. At the beginning of the Civil War, the Union had no military balloon corps. Civilian aerialists quickly offered their services to the federal government, however. Military commanders gave the balloonists a mixed reception. Some commanders liked the idea and found ways to make use of balloons. Others remained skeptical. They resisted the technology and viewed setbacks as failures.

Perhaps the best-known balloonist aiding the Union was Thaddeus Sobieski Constantine Lowe, a Pennsylvania aeronaut. Lowe was a showman. He used his balloons to draw crowds at fairs, civic celebrations, and other large gatherings. Before the war, Lowe unsuccessfully attempted to cross the Atlantic Ocean in a balloon. After the fall of Fort Sumter, the patriotic balloonist went to the nation's capital and offered the government his equipment and expertise. Some military commanders may have failed to see the value of aerial reconnaissance, but the experienced aviator knew that he could contribute to the war effort. Lowe made a dramatic impression on June 18, 1861, when he demonstrated the value of his balloon. President Abraham Lincoln was in his office in the Executive Mansion (now called the

White House) when he received a telegram from Lowe. Historian Robert V. Bruce recorded it this way:

> To the President of the United States
>
> Sir: This point of observation commands an area nearly 50 miles in diameter. The city, with its girdle of encampments, presents a superb scene. I have pleasure in sending you this first dispatch ever telegraphed from an aerial station, and in acknowledging indebtedness for your encouragement for the opportunity of demonstrating the availability of the science of aeronautics in the military service of the country.
>
> T.S.C. Lowe

Lowe's theatrics worked. Although other aeronauts competed for and occasionally received opportunities to work with the Army, Lincoln created the Union Army Corps and named Thaddeus Lowe its chief aeronaut.

Lowe used hydrogen balloons. He preferred the lifting power of the lighter-than-air gas to hot air. To produce his hydrogen, the balloonist used two large generators that held iron filings. Workers slowly added sulfuric acid to the iron filings, and the resulting chemical reaction produced hydrogen. The other generator cooled the hydrogen and removed other gases. Using this process, it took a few hours to fill a balloon. Lowe mounted his hydrogen-producing generators on wagons that followed the balloon force as it traveled from place to place. To start, the balloon crew laid out a large ground cloth to protect the balloon. The workers then laid the uninflated balloon on top of the cloth. When all was ready, the crew fired up the generators and filled the balloon with hydrogen. Lowe's mobile generators gave him the ability to transport his balloons in coordination with the Army.

Scouts or officers in airborne balloons gathered useful information for their commanders. The balloonists calculated the size of enemy forces by counting campfires at night or tents during the day. The men in the air discovered where the enemy's lines were. They even determined whether reinforcements were on their way. Observers learned that fast-moving dust clouds in the distance usually meant that cavalry was on the way. Slow-moving clouds meant infantry. Union balloonists ascended in red-white-and-blue wicker baskets. Balloonists decorated their balloons with distinctive colors. By doing this, they established a tradition that is carried on by today's military aviators, who adorn their craft with decals and mascots.

To relay information to the ground without returning to earth, observers used three different methods. Sometimes the balloonists signaled to those on the ground. Some wrote or drew their observations and dropped them as weighted messages. In still other instances, balloonists sent their messages back to earth via the telegraph. Balloon scouts even developed their own telegraph code to reduce the time needed to translate the messages from Morse code.

As early as May 1861, Southern balloonists approached the Confederate government about using balloons to help the military. In mid-to-late June of that year, there were several unconfirmed reports of balloons behind Confederate lines in northern Virginia. The accuracy of these reports has never been determined. General Beauregard was the Confederate commander in northern Virginia at that time, however. When he later approved the use of the *Hunley* submarine in Charleston Bay, he demonstrated that he was willing to try unconventional methods and weapons.

General Joseph Johnston used a balloon during the Peninsular Campaign for scouting purposes. Lacking the resources that the North enjoyed, the Confederates made their balloon out of cotton and coated it with tar to prevent leaks. A young captain named John Randolph Bryan volunteered for scouting duty before learning that the order involved riding in a balloon.

Bryan begged to return to his command, but Johnston ordered the captain into the air. The first attempt nearly killed him. The crew filled the balloon with hot air by burning pine knots and turpentine. This hardly gave the balloon enough lift to rise. Furthermore, only one rope secured the balloon to the ground. The heavy balloon rose slowly into the sky. Up in the balloon, the petrified Bryan was exposed to Union artillery and sharpshooters. In the air, the balloon whirled around and around its single mooring line.

Bryan did his best. He recorded troop locations and estimated the troops' sizes. Then, as the air in the balloon cooled, it began to descend. The ground crew helped by pulling the heavy craft down by hand. The descent was painfully slow, however. Union artillery fired at the balloonist and his craft. The Confederate crew made modifications to their system for subsequent attempts. To allow the balloon to descend more rapidly, the crew used a team of six horses to haul in the mooring rope. The Confederates also relocated their ascension site each time, as a precaution against Union artillery.

Balloonists on both sides shared several common experiences. These included attracting the attention of enemy sharpshooters and artillery crews. Although the balloons often went up well behind lines, these highly visible craft inevitably drew enemy fire. Northern and Southern balloonists also suffered at the hands of military officers who doubted the value of ballooning. As noted, some commanders did not trust the technology and saw no benefit to such ventures. At times, unfavorable weather conditions such as high winds or rainy weather prevented the balloons from being much help. Aerial observations aided the Union on several occasions during the first two years of fighting, however. The Confederates despised the Union balloons because their presence in the air forced artillery and infantry units to take steps to avoid detection.

President Lincoln rotated his commanding generals as he searched for a leader capable of victory. Because of these

President Abraham Lincoln created a special balloon corps for the Union. Balloonists were responsible for monitoring enemy camps and movement at great distances by counting campfires and measuring dust clouds. Above, Lowe observes a battle from the basket of one of his hot-air balloons.

changes, the balloon corps suffered. As the Army of the Potomac moved toward the pivotal Battle of Gettysburg (July 1–3, 1863), Union troops did not bring balloons with them from Washington. In large part, this was because of a change in the generalship.

As the war dragged on, the South lacked the resources to maintain a balloon corps. In fact, the demands of war made it difficult for either side to continue its aerial exploits. As author Donald E. Markle explains, "The result was that while both the Union and the Confederacy were interested in the use of the hot air balloon, reality soon set in and both sides abandoned the projects."

The Union disbanded its balloon corps in August 1863. Although balloons did not play a major role in the Civil War, later versions of the inflatable craft were used in subsequent wars. Perhaps more importantly, the limited success of balloons demonstrated the value of aerial photography, both during war and for national defense in peacetime.

CRYPTOLOGY

Another area in which technology was used during the Civil War was espionage. Spies on both sides gathered information and communicated with their superiors. The telegraph was the fastest way to transmit information. It was not difficult for either side to tap into telegraph lines and intercept messages, however. To offset this wiretapping, the Union and Confederacy encoded their messages. Cryptography, or writing in codes, is an ancient craft. The purpose is simple: Encode a message in a way that will allow the intended recipient to understand it and deny others the ability to read it. Code cracking, called cryptanalysis, is almost as old as cryptography, however. Code writing and code cracking together make up the field of cryptology.

The North enjoyed more success in cryptology than did the South. There are several explanations for this. First, the South managed to gather intelligence effectively by other means. Especially in the early part of the war, the Confederates' dominant cavalry helped to gather and send intelligence. As a result of this sort of success, Confederate officials never seemed to grasp the importance of developing secure codes or supporting efforts to crack Union codes.

Second, Union armies did not reach deep into the South until later in the war. This meant that as the war progressed, the Union's chances of intercepting Southern messages increased, and the need for Union cryptology efforts intensified.

Third, the Union had at least three gifted code breakers: David Homer Bates, Albert A. Chandler, and Charles A. Tinker. Each of these men was young, energetic, and had a knack for deciphering enemy codes. The three worked in the telegraph room of the War Department. President Lincoln, a frequent visitor there, often observed them as they worked. Finally, the South did not use a uniform code system. In contrast, the North took several steps to set up and protect their code.

Confederate codes were relatively simple. The South used several different methods. The first was the dictionary code. General Albert Sydney Johnston corresponded with Confederate president Jefferson Davis using this method. In a dictionary code, a coded number that designates a word's location in a specific dictionary replaces each word in the message. Thus, the word *scout* might be encoded as "311-1-9," for page 311, column 1, and word 9. To use this code, the sender and the recipient of the message needed to have identical copies of the chosen dictionary.

Another cipher used in the South was called the "Caesar." This system replaces each letter by the third letter that follows it in the alphabet. The coded messages appear as meaningless nonsense, but the code is simple and easily broken. The South used other methods, as well. Some were more advanced but still were primitive when compared to Union cryptography. When Northern code breakers deciphered the Southern codes, it enabled the Union to gain critical information about Confederate movements, plans, and locations.

The most advanced form of encryption technology used in the war was the route cipher. Developed by Union cryptographers, the route cipher is a machine that writes the message out while reorganizing it in a rectangle frame of stated dimensions. Instead of mixing up the letters, the route cipher jumbles the words. In a route cipher, the coded message includes the key to understanding the message. The key word indicates the size of the column and the route of the message. To decipher the message, the recipient reads it using the key included in the text. The reader begins with the key word and follows the message using the route specified.

Union operatives complicated route cipher messages further by encoding the key words. Intercepted messages were readable, but they were impossible to understand without the key. The Confederate government printed copies of captured Union ciphers in Southern newspapers and offered rewards for their successful decipherment. The Union code survived the war intact, however. By incorporating the route cipher with code words, the North effectively preventing the South from cracking the code.

Technology's Impact After the War

The U.S. Civil War helped chart the course for the kind of nation the United States became: a nation committed to equality for all and one that protects the rights of each individual. With the Civil War, the tension between states' rights and federal power was finally resolved. The war also pointed the way toward settling issues of equality that were dealt with more fully in the century that followed.

In addition, the Civil War remains the central event in the nation's history because of the role that technology played in the war. It is important to note that many of the inventions that were tested during the struggle did not affect the outcome of the war. Nevertheless, it is equally important to note that many of those same technological advances laid the foundations for modern life. In that sense, the technologies of the Civil War are as central to the history of the United States as the political values.

The importance of technology was apparent during the war. That importance could be seen even more plainly after the

A War of Firsts

The Civil War boasted numerous "firsts" in war, many of which relied on the latest technologies. Author Burke Davis lists many of these first-time technologies. They include:

- railroad artillery
- a successful submarine
- a "snorkel" breathing device
- the periscope, used for trench warfare
- land-mine fields
- military telegraph
- naval torpedoes
- aerial reconnaissance
- antiaircraft fire
- telescopic sights for rifles
- fixed ammunition
- ironclad navies
- a steel ship
- revolving gun turrets
- military railroads
- a workable machine gun
- electrically exploded bombs and torpedoes

Most of these technologies did not change the outcome of the Civil War. The innovations led to improved offspring, however. Many of those later devices featured improvements that accomplished things that the inventors of the 1860s only dreamed could be possible.

war. The growth of technology since the Civil War demonstrates the value of technology to the United States. The war made the United States a technological power or, at the very least, positioned the reunited nation to become one. Manufacturing grew dramatically during the war with the push to clothe, feed, and equip the armies in the field. In 1865, at war's end, factories shifted to peacetime production, turning out products for civilians. Steel production grew during the war. Industrialist Andrew Carnegie's steel company provided the steel the nation needed for postwar growth: for the building of railroads and bridges and for increased manufacturing. The United States was changing, and the Civil War was the instrument that set much of the change into motion.

A year after the war ended, the first transatlantic telegraph cable was laid across the bottom of the Atlantic Ocean. America now enjoyed direct and almost immediate communication with Europe. Four years after General Lee's April 1865 surrender to General Grant at Appomattox, the first transcontinental railroad was completed. With the driving of a ceremonial golden spike, the East Coast was linked by rail to the Pacific Ocean. By 1890, four more rail lines connected the two coasts. New railroads also invaded the South, increasing its track mileage significantly in the 25 years after the war.

The expansion of railroads across the Great Plains encouraged settlement of the vast, open spaces west of the Missouri River. Many Europeans sailed to America to build new lives and settled on the Great Plains. All of this was possible because of an act of Congress passed during the war: the Homestead Act of 1862. The Homestead Act allowed settlers to purchase a 160-acre plot of land for a small surveying fee. The land became theirs for good if they lived on it for five years and made improvements to the property. Additional legislation passed by Congress in the 1870s opened up more land and allowed settlers to acquire larger tracts. This enabled ranchers to make a living on the arid plains. American factories manufactured barbed wire to enclose the once-open plains so that ranchers could graze their cattle.

As settlers populated the plains, the railroad and the telegraph linked them with markets and factories in the East. At the same time, government policies pushed American Indians onto

The technological advancements that occurred during the Civil War continued to push the industrialization of the United States after the fighting had ended. Factories built to produce war supplies were converted for civilian use, and infrastructure development boomed as manufacturing increased. This explosion of production inspired great ideas, projects, and achievements like the transcontinental railroad (above) that have shaped the inventive spirit of the United States.

reservations and opened up their ancestral lands to eager white settlers. By 1900, the United States had more than 200,000 miles of railroad tracks. The railroad companies cooperated with each other. They established standardized times and the time zones we know today. By doing this, the railroads helped to make American life more efficient. Transportation and communication technology made life on the vast and lonely Great Plains more bearable. The United States became a continental power.

Another technological factor in the development of the United States during and immediately after the Civil War was the mechanization of farming. American manufacturer Cyrus McCormick patented his horse-drawn mechanical reaper in

1831. He sold hundreds of thousands of the time-saving devices during and after the war. The postwar economy forced many people into farming and increased the demand for McCormick's reapers.

Together, the development of a transportation infrastructure (a network of roads and railroads), the growth of manufacturing capabilities, and expansion across the Great Plains brought about the urbanization of the United States. By 1910, more Americans lived in cities than in rural areas. Other technologies improved Americans' standard of living. These advances included Thomas Edison's light bulb and Alexander Graham Bell's telephone.

The Civil War marked the end of the terrible institution of slavery, an unjustifiable way of life. The war also marked a major shift in the American mind-set. No longer was America simply a collection of individual states. After the war, the United States were truly united. No longer were Americans content to live as they always had. Instead, they seemed driven to learn more, to accomplish more, and to become great. This drive to become thoroughly modern began to characterize the American spirit. The Civil War was costly, and it opened deep wounds in the national identity, but it also helped the United States to transform itself from the old to the new, from the past to the future, and from the traditional to the modern. The technology of war played a significant role in that process.

Glossary

AERIAL RECONNAISSANCE   Collecting information for military purposes from the air.

ARTILLERY   Cannons or other large guns.

BATTERY   An artillery unit consisting of four to six cannons.

BLOCKADE   Attempt by hostile ships or troops to isolate or block access to a place such as a port or harbor to prevent the entry or exit of people, goods, and materials.

BLOCKADE-RUNNER   Name given to a small, fast ship that attempted to slip through the Union navy's blockade of Southern ports during the Civil War.

BORE   The inside of a gun's barrel.

BREASTWORKS   Defensive barricades, usually about breast-high, erected to shield defenders from enemy fire; sometimes called defensive works or works.

BREECH   The back end of a gun's barrel.

BREECHLOADER   A firearm that is loaded through the breech, or back end, of the weapon.

CALIBER   The precise width of a gun's bore.

CANISTER   An antipersonnel shell fired from a cannon; the tin canister fragmented as it was fired from the cannon and dispersed a large number of iron or steel balls.

ESPIONAGE   Spying on or gathering intelligence about the enemy.

FIELDWORKS   Trenches and other defensive structures constructed by armies.

FLANK The wing or side of a military formation.

FLINTLOCK Mechanism in which a piece of flint strikes a piece of steel, producing a spark to ignite gunpowder to discharge a firearm.

GUN A cannon with a long barrel that fires its shots in a low trajectory.

HOWITZER A cannon with a barrel length shorter than that of a gun and longer than that of a mortar; a howitzer fires its shots in a mid-range trajectory.

INTELLIGENCE Information gathered about the enemy.

IRONCLAD Wooden warship of the nineteenth century that used iron plates to protect the hull.

MINIÉ A rifle bullet that expanded after the initial discharge; this expansion caused the bullet to grip the bore and spin, thus increasing the rifle's range and accuracy.

MORTAR An artillery weapon that fires projectiles in a high arc or trajectory; a mortar's trajectory makes it capable of shelling enemy positions behind breastworks.

MUSKET An early firearm with a smooth bore, usually fired by a flintlock mechanism.

MUZZLE The mouth of the bore of a cannon or firearm.

NAPOLEON A light, short, smoothbore artillery gun similar to a howitzer.

PERCUSSION CAP A metal plate coated with a chemical; when struck with a metal hammer, a percussion cap discharges a firearm.

PICKET An advance guard or outpost that formed a scattered line in advance of an army's main camp.

RAM A device fitted to the reinforced bow of a steam-powered vessel designed to inflict damage on enemy ships by means of a collision.

RAMROD A rod or stick used to push the powder and ball down the barrel of a musket or a muzzle-loading rifle.

RIFLE   A firearm with spiral grooves cut into the barrel's bore to rotate the fired shell.

RIFLED   Word used to describe the barrel of a firearm or artillery piece that features spiral grooves; rifling increases the accuracy and distance of the weapon.

SABER   A cavalry sword.

SHELL   A hollow projectile fired from a cannon and designed to explode after a set amount of time or upon impact.

SHRAPNEL   A hollow metal shell filled with lead shot and outfitted with a percussion or time-delay fuse; detonation of the cap or fuse scatters the shot. Sometimes called case shot or spherical case shot.

SMOOTHBORE   Word used to describe a firearm in which the barrel's bore is smooth, with no rifling grooves.

SOLID SHOT   A cannonball cast of solid metal.

SPAR TORPEDO   An explosive payload at the end of a pole attached to the bow of a submarine or semisubmersible ship.

STRATEGY   Wide-ranging goals in military operations that require the use of tactics.

SUBMERSIBLE   A submarine.

TACTICS   Deploying and moving troops before, during, and after combat in order to achieve strategic objectives.

TORPEDO   During the Civil War, a naval mine that either floated in the water or was planted against the intended target.

TRAJECTORY   The flight path of a bullet, shell, or other projectile.

Bibliography

Bacon, Benjamin W. *Sinews of War: How Technology, Industry, and Transportation Won the Civil War.* Novato, Calif.: Presidio Press, 1997.

Bilby, Joseph G. *Civil War Firearms: Their Historical Background, Tactical Use and Modern Collecting and Shooting.* Conshohocken, Pa.: Combined Books, 1996.

Bollet, Alfred Jay. *Civil War Medicine: Challenges and Triumphs.* Tucson, Ariz.: Galen Press, 2002.

Brooks, Stewart. *Civil War Medicine.* Springfield, Ill.: Charles C. Thomas, 1966.

Bruce, Robert V. *Lincoln and the Tools of War.* Indianapolis: Bobbs-Merrill, 1956.

Catton, Bruce. *The American Heritage New History of the Civil War.* New York: American Heritage, 1996.

Clark, John E., Jr. *Railroads in the Civil War: The Impact of Management on Victory and Defeat.* Baton Rouge: Louisiana State University Press, 2001.

D'Aoustand, Maurice. "Hoodwinked During America's Civil War: Union Military Deception." *Civil War Times Magazine* (May 2006).

Davis, Burke. *The Civil War: Strange & Fascinating Facts.* New York: The Fairfax Press, 1982.

DeKay, James Tertius. Monitor: *The Story of the Legendary Civil War Ironclad and the Man Whose Invention Changed the Course of History.* New York: Ballantine Books, 1997.

Dickey, Thomas S., and George C. Peter. *Field Artillery Projectiles of the American Civil War.* Mechanicsville, Va.: Arsenal Publications II, 1993.

Drury, Ian, and Tony Gibbons. *The Civil War Military Machine: Weapons and Tactics of the Union and Confederate Armed Forces.* New York: Smithmark Publishers, 1993.

Evans, Charles M. *The War of Aeronauts: A History of Ballooning During the Civil War*. Mechanicsburg, Pa.: Stackpole Books, 2002.

Freemon, Frank R. *Gangrene and Glory: Medical Care During the American Civil War*. Madison, N.J.: Fairleigh Dickinson University Press, 1998.

———. *Microbes and Minié Balls: An Annotated Bibliography of Civil War Medicine*. Rutherford, N.J.: Fairleigh Dickinson University Press, 1993.

Griffith, Paddy. *Battle Tactics of the Civil War*. New Haven: Yale University Press, 1987.

Haydon, F. Stansbury. *Military Ballooning During the Early Civil War*. Baltimore: The Johns Hopkins University Press, 1941.

Hill, Richard. *War at Sea in the Ironclad Age*. London: Cassell, 2000.

Jones, Archer. *Civil War Command and Strategy: The Process of Victory and Defeat*. New York: Free Press, 1992.

Lee, James C. "The Undertaker's Role During the American Civil War." *Civil War Times* (November 1996).

Markle, Donald E. *Spies and Spymasters of the Civil War*. New York: Barnes and Noble Books, 1994.

McAulay, John D. *Civil War Breech Loading Rifles: A Survey of the Innovative Infantry Arms of the American Civil War*. Lincoln, R.I.: Andrew Mowbray, Inc., 1987.

McPherson, James M. *Battle Cry of Freedom: The Civil War Era*. Oxford: Oxford University Press, 1988.

———. *Ordeal by Fire: The Civil War and Reconstruction*. New York: Alfred A. Knopf, 1982.

Mindell, David A. *War, Technology, and Experience Aboard the USS Monitor*. Baltimore: The Johns Hopkins University Press, 2000.

Parish, Peter J. *The American Civil War*. New York: Holmes and Meier Publishers, 1975.

Ragan, Mark K. *Submarine Warfare in the Civil War*. Cambridge, Mass.: De Capo Press, 2002.

Roberts, William H. *Civil War Ironclads: The U.S. Navy and Industrial Mobilization*. Baltimore: The Johns Hopkins University Press, 2002.

———. *USS New Ironsides in the Civil War*. Annapolis, Md.: Naval Institute Press, 1999.

Ross, Charles D. *Trial by Fire: Science, Technology, and the Civil War.* Shippensburg, Pa.: White Mane Books, 2000.

Rutkow, Ira M. *Bleeding Blue and Gray: Civil War Strategy and the Evolution of American Medicine.* New York: Random House, 2005.

Silverstone, Paul H. *Warships of the Civil War Navies.* Annapolis, Md.: Naval Institute Press, 1989.

Smith, George Winston. *Medicines for the Union Army: The United States Army Laboratories During the Civil War.* Madison, Wis.: American Institute of the History of Pharmacy, 1962.

Smith, Graham. *Warman's Civil War Weapons.* Iola, Wis.: KP Books, 2005.

Trotter, William R. *Ironclads and Columbiads: The Civil War in North Carolina: The Coast.* Winston-Salem, N.C.: John F. Blair, 1989.

Vandiver, Frank E. *Rebel Brass: The Confederate Command System.* Baton Rouge: Louisiana State University Press, 1956.

Walker, Sally M. *Secrets of a Civil War Submarine: Solving the Mysteries of the H.L. Hunley.* Minneapolis, Minn.: Carolrhoda Books, 2005.

Whisker, James Biser. *U.S. and Confederate Arms and Armories During the American Civil War* (Volumes 1–4). Lewiston, N.Y.: The Edwin Mellen Press, 2002.

Wilbur, C. Keith. *Civil War Medicine: 1861–1865.* Old Saybrook, Conn.: The Globe Pequot Press, 1998.

WEB SITES

http://www.history.navy.mil/danfs/i2/intellig.htm

http://www.navsource.org/archives/08/01idx.htm

http://www.navyandmarine.org/alligator/

http://www.pbs.org/wgbh/nova/lostsub/hist1861n07.html

http://www.onr.navy.mil/Focus/blowballast/sub/history3.htm

Further Resources

Katcher, Philip. *Sharpshooters of the Civil War*. Chicago: Raintree, 2003.

Lieurance, Suzanne. *Weapons and Strategies of the Civil War*. Berkeley Heights, N.J.: Enslow Publishers, 2004.

Nardo, Don. *The Civil War*. San Diego: Lucent Books, 2003.

Stewart, Gail B. *Weapons of War*. San Diego: Lucent Books, 2000.

WEB SITES

Civil War Submarines
http://americancivilwar.com/tcwn/civil_war/naval_submarine.html

The Eli Whitney Museum & Workshop: The Cotton Gin
http://www.eliwhitney.org/cotton.htm

Friends of the *Hunley*
http://www.hunley.org

The Hunt for the Alligator
http://sanctuaries.noaa.gov/alligator/

The Mariners' Museum, Newport News, Virginia
http://www.mariner.org/

National Museum of Civil War Medicine: Museum Exhibits
http://www.civilwarmed.org/exhibits.cfm

National Underwater and Marine Agency: CSS *Hunley*
http://www.numa.net/expeditions/hunley.html

Picture Credits

Index

About
the Authors

SHANE MOUNTJOY resides in York, Nebraska, where he is associate professor of history and dean of students at York College. Recognized by his peers and students as an outstanding teacher, Professor Mountjoy insists that he is still just a student at heart. He has earned degrees from York College, Lubbock Christian University, the University of Nebraska, and the University of Missouri. He and his wife homeschool their four daughters, Macy, Karlie, Ainsley, and Tessa. He is the author of several books, including *Causes of the Civil War*, another title in the series THE CIVIL WAR: A NATION DIVIDED.

TIM MCNEESE is associate professor of history at York College in York, Nebraska, where he is in his seventeenth year of college instruction. Professor McNeese earned an associate of arts degree from York College, a bachelor of arts in history and political science from Harding University, and a master of arts in history from Missouri State University. A prolific author of books for elementary, middle and high school, and college readers, McNeese has published more than 100 books and educational materials over the past 20 years, on everything from the founding of early New York to Hispanic authors. His writing has earned him a citation in the library reference work *Contemporary Authors*, and multiple citations in *Best Books for Young Teen Readers*. In 2006, McNeese appeared on the History Channel program *Risk Takers, History Makers: John Wesley Powell and the Grand Canyon*. He was a faculty member at the 2006 Tony Hillerman Writers Conference in Albuquerque. His wife, Beverly, is an assistant professor of English at York College. They have two married children, Noah and Summer, and three grandchildren, Ethan, Adrianna, and Finn William. Tim and Bev McNeese sponsored study trips for college students on the Lewis and Clark Trail in 2003 and 2005 and to the American Southwest in 2008. You may contact Professor McNeese at tdmcneese@york.edu.